D0781552

Paul Virilio is an innovative figure in the study of architecture, space, and the city. *Virilio for Architects* primes readers for their first encounter with his crucial texts on some of the vital theoretical debates of the twenty-first century, including:

- oblique architecture and bunker archeology;
- critical space and the overexposed city;
- the ultracity and very high buildings;
- grey ecology and global hypermovement.

In exploring Virilio's most important architectural ideas and their impact, John Armitage traces his engagement with other key architectural and scientific thinkers such as Claude Parent, Benoît B. Mandelbrot, and Bernard Tschumi. *Virilio for Architects* allows students, researchers, and non-academic readers to connect with Virilio's distinctive architectural theories, critical studies, and fresh ideas.

John Armitage is Professor of Media Arts at Winchester School of Art, University of Southampton. He is the author and editor of numerous books on the work of Paul Virilio, including *Virilio and the Media* and *The Virilio Dictionary*.

Thinkers for Architects

Series Editor: Adam Sharr, Newcastle University, UK

Editorial Board

Jonathan A. Hale, University of Nottingham, UK
Hilde Heynen, KU Leuven, Netherlands
David Leatherbarrow, University of Pennsylvania, USA

Architects have often looked to philosophers and theorists from beyond the discipline for design inspiration or in search of a critical framework for practice. This original series offers quick, clear introductions to key thinkers who have written about architecture and whose work can yield insights for designers.

'Each unintimidatingly slim book makes sense of the subjects' complex theories.'

Building Design

'. . . a valuable addition to any studio space or computer lab.'

Architectural Record

'. . . a creditable attempt to present their subjects in a useful way.'

Architectural Review

Virilio for Architects
John Armitage

Baudrillard for Architects
Francesco Proto

Kant for Architects
Diane Morgan

Merleau-Ponty for Architects
Jonathan Hale

Virilio

for

Architects

John Armitage

Routledge
Taylor & Francis Group

LONDON AND NEW YORK

First published 2015
by Routledge
2 Park Square, Milton Park, Abingdon, Oxon OX14 4RN

and by Routledge
711 Third Avenue, New York, NY 10017

Routledge is an imprint of the Taylor & Francis Group, an informa business

© 2015 John Armitage

British Library Cataloguing-in-Publication Data
A catalogue record for this book is available from the British Library

Library of Congress Cataloging-in-Publication Data
Armitage, John, 1956–
    Virilio for architects / John Armitage.
        pages cm. — (Thinkers for architects)
    Includes bibliographical references and index.
    1. Virilio, Paul. 2. Architecture—Philosophy. I. Title.
    HM479.V57A895 2015
    720.1—dc23   2015000986

ISBN: 978-0-415-81902-2 (hbk)
ISBN: 978-0-415-81903-9 (pbk)
ISBN: 978-1-315-73069-1 (ebk)

Typeset in Frutiger
by Keystroke, Station Road, Codsall, Wolverhampton

Printed and bound in Great Britain by
TJ International Ltd, Padstow, Cornwall

Contents

Series editor's preface

Adam Sharr

Architects have often looked to thinkers in philosophy and theory for design ideas, or in search of a critical framework for practice. Yet architects and students of architecture can struggle to navigate thinkers' writings. It can be daunting to approach original texts with little appreciation of their contexts. And existing introductions seldom explore a thinker's architectural material in any detail. This original series offers clear, quick and accurate introductions to key thinkers who have written about architecture. Each book summarizes what a thinker has to offer for architects. It locates their architectural thinking in the body of their work, introduces significant books and essays, helps decode terms and provides quick reference for further reading. If you find philosophical and theoretical writing about architecture difficult, or just don't know where to begin, this series will be indispensable.

Books in the *Thinkers for Architects* series come out of architecture. They pursue architectural modes of understanding, aiming to introduce a thinker to an architectural audience. Each thinker has a unique and distinctive ethos, and the structure of each book derives from the character at its focus. The thinkers explored are prodigious writers and any short introduction can only address a fraction of their work. Each author – an architect or an architectural critic – has focused on a selection of a thinker's writings which they judge most relevant to designers and interpreters of architecture. Inevitably, much will be left out. These books will be the first point of reference, rather than the last word, about a particular thinker for architects. It is hoped that they will encourage you to read further, offering an incentive to delve deeper into the original writings of a particular thinker.

The *Thinkers for Architects* series has proved highly successful, expanding now to twelve volumes dealing with familiar cultural figures whose writings have influenced architectural designers, critics and commentators in distinctive and important ways. Books explore the work of: Gilles Deleuze and Felix Guattari, Martin Heidegger, Luce Irigaray, Homi Bhabha, Pierre Bourdieu, Walter Benjamin, Jacques Derrida, Hans-Georg Gadamer, Michael Foucault, Nelson Goodman and Henri Lefebvre. Unusually, this book on Paul Virilio addresses the work of a thinker who began with architecture before moving on to cultural theory. Future volumes are projected, addressing the work of Jean Baudrillard, Immanuel Kant and Maurice Merleau-Ponty. The series continues to expand, addressing an increasingly rich diversity of contemporary thinkers who have something to say to architects.

Adam Sharr is Professor of Architecture at the University of Newcastle upon Tyne; Principal of Adam Sharr Architects; and Editor of *arq: Architectural Research Quarterly*, a Cambridge University Press international architecture journal. His books published by Routledge include *Heidegger for Architects* and *Reading Architecture and Culture*.

Illustration credits

1. Paul Virilio, L'Argoat Bar and Restaurant, La Rochelle, France, 22 May 2009. Image courtesy of the author (p. xiv).

2. Analysing the oblique

   2. The oblique Church of Sainte-Bernadette du Banlay, Nevers, France, 2006: west elevation. Image courtesy of the author (p. 24).

   3. The oblique Church of Sainte-Bernadette du Banlay, Nevers, France, 2006: east elevation. Image courtesy of the author (p. 25).

   4. The oblique Church of Sainte-Bernadette du Banlay, Nevers, France, 2006: south elevation. Image courtesy of the author (p. 25).

   5. The oblique Church of Sainte-Bernadette du Banlay, Nevers, France, 2006: interior view of the altar. Image courtesy of the author (p. 26).

   6. The oblique Church of Sainte-Bernadette du Banlay, Nevers, France, 2006: interior with tapestries decorating the concrete wall. Image courtesy of the author (p. 26).

   7. The oblique Church of Sainte-Bernadette du Banlay, Nevers, France, 2006: north elevation. Image courtesy of the author (p. 27).

   8. 'Observation post revealed by the erosion of the dunes', from Paul Virilio's *Bunker Archeology* (1994a: 173). Image courtesy of Paul Virilio and Princeton Architectural Press (p. 31).

Acknowledgements

I am grateful to Adam Sharr and to Fran Ford for their intellectual and editorial support for this book. Paul Virilio, Dan Simon at Princeton Architectural Press, and Colin Spoelman at Bernard Tschumi Architects, New York, kindly permitted me to reproduce photographs. Finally, I offer a heartfelt thank you to my partner Joanne Roberts for her continuing love, insights, and understanding.

Figure 1 Paul Virilio, L'Argoat Bar and Restaurant, La Rochelle, France, 22 May 2009.

CHAPTER 1

Introduction

Paul Virilio's chief contribution to French post-Second World War thinking has been to demonstrate that questions of architecture are urban and military questions. For him, architecture is not something just to appreciate or study; it is also a critical site of cultural action and intervention where territorial and military relations are both established and possibly unsettled. Virilio is a rare intellectual, in the sense that his writings have made a difference both to theoretical debates on architecture and to the making of architecture (Virilio and Parent 1997a, 1997b, 1997c). Architecture Principe, for many Virilio's most remarkable creation – an architectural group and its eponymous magazine, *Architecture Principe* – not only included the famous French architect Claude Parent; it also introduced the theory of 'the oblique function', which resulted in the construction of a major architectural work – the Church of Sainte-Bernadette du Banlay in Nevers in 1966 (Virilio and Parent 1996).

Yet Virilio is not a political activist, who uses direct action, such as demonstrating or striking in opposition to or support of a cause, masquerading as an architectural thinker. He is unconvinced by the idea that intellectual architectural groups and architecture journals can or should assemble, marshal, or coordinate the general population – for example, for the purpose of resisting the militarization of urban space. This is because Virilio does not believe either that there is such a thing as *the* general population – in the sense of a pure, genuine, united community – or that there may be a quick solution to spatial inequality, some way of fixing it for good, at some indeterminate time in the future. Space, Virilio argues, is a site of *ongoing* critique and struggle that can never be certain for one side or the other. In this sense, Virilio's intellectual contribution has been not only to expose the militarization of urban architecture, but also to show that this architecture is never reducible to militarization.

For Virilio, the study of architecture involves exposing the relations of urban and military power that exist within culture at any given moment, so that we may then consider how marginal or subordinate groups might win architectural space, however fleetingly, from the dominant group (Virilio and Brausch 1993). This is an enormously multifaceted process, full of potential drawbacks, and we will examine below in greater detail how, for instance, Virilio has theorized the computer interface, virtual space, and the 'contamination' of real space and put into practice this approach. For now, though, concentrating on the relations of urban and military power suggests a way of thinking about Virilio's conception of virtual and real spaces. However, his thought is not a set of internally coherent, unchanging ideas through which we can move step by step, from the unity of urban time and place to 'the overexposed city', or chapter by chapter, from real space to virtual space; it is rather an enduring and unavoidably incomplete process, always recombining and redividing. Avoiding a philosophical standpoint founded upon a belief in a historical point of pure origin, what is important about Virilio's contingent architectural thought is that it is focused upon a critique of the binary oppositions that endow a first term in a sequence – such as real space/virtual space – with the authority of a governing fixed point. Virilio does not become interested, for example, in theories of reception and perception just because that may seem a good idea at the time; his thinking forms part of a response to architectural, urban, and military developments at exact moments in French post-Second World War history (e.g. in the early 1980s, which saw the transformation of real space into virtual space). As Virilio might put it, he is not interested in architectural theory and practice per se. He is interested in why they were as they were in the 1950s or 1960s or are as they are in the 2000s. For Virilio, architecture is a process over which we must mount a critique and a struggle against unequal interactions of urban and military power – not a stationary object that we can merely explain or wrap up in a grand overarching theory.

In this context, the role of the intellectual-architect is, as Virilio puts it, relatively inactive politically. Speaking on the subject of the intellectual-architect in the 1990s, Virilio pointed to the 'disqualification' of the architectural critic who becomes embroiled in political activism: 'To me the work of a thinker consists of his work, not his opinions. To me opinions are nothing. So to consider opinions of primary importance is to disqualify the work' (Virilio and Brügger 2001: 94).

At the same time, Virilio also stresses that intellectual-architects do raise important urban, military, and *architectural* questions. Intellectual-architects, he argues, are also people who question whose urban visions are represented and whose are not. Moreover, unless we operate within the tensions between an intellectual-architect's politics, critical works, and thought, we will never know what architectural studies can and cannot do, visualize, and represent in the urban realm; nor will we know what they have to do politically or what they alone have a privileged ability to do architecturally. Intellectual-architects, Virilio suggests, are not just concerned about the declining influence of architectural critics; they are also concerned about the architecture and urbanism of 'the big night' (e.g. the silence surrounding the disappearance of the night sky in contemporary cities) and the decline of certain forms of urban stasis (through the emergence of various forms of escape from the city). The intellectual-as-architect example points at once to Virilio's sense of the limitations and *relevance* of intellectual work and to his commitment to architectural studies as urban and military studies.

Virilio's architectural career

Anyone beginning to write a history of the French post-Second World War intellectual architectural scene, and looking around for some archetypal urban figure to connect its numerous avant-garde trends and ideological phases, would find himself or herself almost spontaneously turning to Paul Virilio. In the 1950s Virilio played a key role within a group of French architects concerned with the significance of military strategy for the development of the modern city. In the 1960s and 1970s he appeared as a foremost exponent in various new intellectual and architectural fields: architectural studies of destruction and acceleration, technology, movement, and politics. In the 1980s he was one of the most outspoken and persuasive public – yet intensely private – intellectuals and architects in debates on structural design, the transformation of the modern city, transit, and space. Meanwhile, since the 1990s, Virilio's influential writings on architecture, 'grey ecology', and 'the cities of the beyond', combined with the growing reputation, within and outside the architectural academy, of his work on critical space, globalization, migration, and the event, have earned him global recognition as a pre-eminent figure in architectural studies today.

Virilio's influential writings . . . have earned him global recognition as a pre-eminent figure in architectural studies today.

However, Virilio himself would question any characterization of his architectural career that does not emphasize issues concerning his lack of formal architectural education, the city, war, and large-scale obliteration:

> I don't have any training in architecture whatsoever. I came to the question of the city through the question of war . . . I lived through the trauma of full-scale war, the destruction of cities, like Nantes, where I lived and where eight thousand buildings were destroyed. It was this relationship with war which led me to become interested in the city and in architecture.
>
> (Virilio and Limon 2001: 51)

These remarks present students of Virilio's work with specific problems – namely how to create an architectural narrative of Virilio, how to introduce his architectural writing on the city, and how to foreground his importance regarding the effects of war and destruction on the field of architecture.

Strangely perhaps (given the problems above), the best way of solving them is to begin with a consideration of Virilio's participation in interviews. For, during the 1980s, 1990s, and beyond, Virilio repeatedly used interviews as a platform for theorizing: not for presenting architectural explanations but for exploring architecture as an oblique concept (see Chapter 2).

Born in Paris in 1932, Virilio grew up in the care of a Breton Catholic mother and a father who was an Italian communist and an illegal alien in France. Virilio has described this dual nationality upbringing in an environment torn apart by the Second World War as one of devastation. He felt estranged from the North Atlantic region in Nantes because of his origins in Paris, from which he was evacuated during the war, and his growing sense of being a 'war baby' (as he often put it) was mainly due to the fact that he was only 15 when Allied bombs fell on Nantes, where his family had sought refuge. For this eventual urban planner and architect, the destruction of the metropolitan setting of Nantes was his testing ground, the fragility of the city his first concern. Eager to escape from Nantes after the Allies liberated France from German occupation in 1945, Virilio returned to Paris and attended the École des Métiers d'Art with the idea of becoming a master artist in stained glass. The frequency with which he has returned to document his early childhood experiences in France during the Second World War signifies their important formative influence on his later thinking, most especially perhaps in terms of his intellectual preoccupation with architecture, urbanism, and militarism.

Architectural studies take on a different character when considered from the standpoint of Virilio's early life. If Virilio was central to the founding of an avant-garde architectural field in France, then that was partly the result of insights afforded by his oblique, equivocal relationship to prevailing ideas of war and the city, art, and architecture. His background as a devout Christian associated with Abbé Pierre (1912–2007) – the French Catholic priest, member of the Resistance during the Second World War, and deputy of the Popular Republican Movement – and with the homeless placed Virilio at an oblique angle to the Second World War, to France, and to French architecture from the 1950s onwards. It might be said of Virilio that he feels better taking a sighting of the domain of architecture from the German bunkers of the Second World War's 'Atlantic Wall' (a massive coastal defensive structure built on Hitler's orders that stretched from Norway through France to Spain) than from French post-Second World War architecture. It was this military perspective that, in an earlier period of his career, allowed him to contest some of the most taken-for-granted features of French cultural and political life (he actively took part in the student-led strikes of Paris in May 1968), while opening architecture up to the submerged questions of the military's relationship to urbanization. Considered within this context, Virilio's importance as an architectural thinker has less to do with his lack of formal architectural education than with how he calls into question the very idea of a purely architectural education. One of the traits of his architectural work is its refusal of the two fundamental directions of Euclidian space – the vertical and the horizontal – of both post-Second World War French architecture and modern American architectural formations such as skyscrapers more generally. In the chapters that follow, Virilio will be seen arguing that, from Manhattan to Marseilles, there is no modern architecture that is not haunted by 'the oblique function' and by 'bunker archeology' (see Chapter 2); no conception of urban space that is free of critical overexposure to the interface of virtual space (see Chapter 3); no city without its increasing nocturnal extremes (see Chapter 4); no architect untouched by 'grey ecology' and 'the cities of the beyond' (see Chapter 5).

Virilio's importance as an architectural thinker has less to do with his lack of formal architectural education than with how he calls into question the very idea of a purely architectural education.

After returning to Paris to work on stained glass in the early post-Second World War years, Virilio eventually deserted his initial vocation, feeling that he could no longer address the theoretical urban and military questions that were starting to consume him in pure practical terms. Significantly, these were also the years in which Virilio became involved in new movements taking shape within French architecture – movements that argued for a more urbanized and militarized conception of architecture and a more architectural conception of urban and military questions.

During his time as founder, with Claude Parent, of the Architecture Principe group, and as editor of its review *Architecture Principe*, Virilio supported himself financially by becoming a discussant, provocateur, writer, and theorist in Parent's architectural practice and elsewhere in Paris. This marked the start of a career that would span nearly 40 years and is thought by many to be a fundamental facet of Virilio's contribution to post-Second World War French architecture, urbanism, and the critique of militarism (see Scalbert and Mostafavi 1996).

Between the 1960s and the 1990s Virilio worked first in Parent's architectural practice and second, crucially, in higher education from 1969 on, as professor and workshop director at the École Spéciale d'Architecture (ESA) in Paris, where he became director of studies in 1973. He also remained a prominent member of the editorial staff of the review *Esprit*. Unlike the writings of other architectural thinkers, which circulate almost exclusively in academic circles, Virilio's editorial and other work has appealed to a much wider audience. Indeed, his ideas have been disseminated on DVD, as in the case of *Penser la vitesse* (Virilio and Paoli 2009); on television (Virilio and Kittler 2001); in the news print media of Western Europe (*La Libération*, *Die Tageszeitung*); and by prestigious university presses such as Princeton (see Virilio 1994a and 2000b). Virilio is a teacher, a curator of exhibitions, and an artist-researcher as much as he is a writer, and his editorial and public influence extends far beyond his post-1975 general directorship of the ESA and those texts he himself has authored.

Despite a lifetime of teaching at the ESA in Paris, it is notable that Virilio has always worked outside traditional architectural academic institutions. While at the ESA, he founded, with Alain Joxe, the Interdisciplinary Center for Research into Peace and Strategic Studies at the House of the Human Sciences, teaching geopolitics: a unique post in France in 1979. He then wrote *L'Insécurité du territoire* (Virilio 1976) and *Speed & Politics: An Essay on Dromology* (Virilio 1986), both essays on geopolitics, militarization, and the new information and communications technology revolution in transport and transmission. Moving to *Popular Defense and Ecological Struggles* (Virilio 1990), he sketched the conditions for popular resistance to war before writing *The Aesthetics of Disappearance* (Virilio 2009a), an essay on the cultural effects of cinematics. One of the most distinctive aspects of Virilio's work at *Esprit*, *Cause commune*, and *Traverses* was the publication of his research on architecture in various monthlies and reviews such as *L'Autre Journal*, *Critique*, or *Les Temps modernes*, where his architectural ideas and philosophical projects could be read by people in the humanities, the sciences, and the arts.

In 1984 Virilio published *The Lost Dimension* (Virilio 1991), wherein he presented his architectural research into the crisis of the contemporary city (see Chapter 3). *War and Cinema: The Logistics of Perception* (Virilio 1989) was another unorthodox 'Virilian' essay on cinematographic techniques used during the two world wars, as was *Negative Horizon* (Virilio 2005b), which studies the links between speed, politics, and the cultural development of western societies. In 1987, under the initiative of the Ministries of Equipment and Housing and the Organization of Territory and Transport, Virilio was awarded Laureate of Architectural Critique status by the French government for his work as a whole. His research on vision technologies continued with the publication of *The Vision Machine* (Virilio 1994b), which deals with progress in automation – not only in postindustrial production but also in our perception of the world. We should also note that, while Virilio was nominated programme director at the International College of Philosophy in 1989, he was simultaneously writing *Polar Inertia* (Virilio 2000c), an essay on the recent evolution in remote-control technology and the environment. By the 1990s Virilio's influence on architecture and various other subjects knew no boundaries, disciplinary or other, as almost all of his works were continually republished and translated into upwards of 15 languages. Once president of the ESA in 1990, Virilio reached out beyond its confines, to become advisor to the French Pavilion Commission for the Universal Exposition in Seville together with Régis Debray, the well-known French intellectual, journalist, government official, and professor of 'mediology' (see Debray 2004). Writing of the motivations behind the Gulf War of 1990–1, Virilio produced *Desert Screen* (Virilio 2002a), a series of chronicles for European newspapers such as *L'Express* that highlighted the US military's special attraction to war at the speed of light. In 1991 Virilio also served as a member of the scientific advisory board for the Memorial of the Battle of Normandy in Caen while additionally preparing an itinerant exhibition for the Ministry of Defence on the theme of 'The City and Its Defenders'. In different ways, Virilio's numerous cultural activities and editorial work with French architects like Henri Gaudin allowed him to break with the pure vocational aspects of higher architectural education and connect with wider aesthetic and political formations beyond the ESA.

In different ways, Virilio's numerous cultural activities and editorial work with French architects like Henri Gaudin allowed him to break with the pure vocational aspects of higher architectural education and connect with wider aesthetic and political formations . . . .

Virilio's research in the 1990s – illustrated for instance by *The Art of the Motor* (Virilio 1995), an essay on the multimedia revolution, and strengthened by his continuing membership of the High Committee for the Housing of Disadvantaged People – has developed out of his long-term fascination with new information and communications technologies; this is evidenced by *Open Sky* (Virilio 1997f), an essay on perspective and real time, optics, and 'grey ecology' (see Chapter 5). Within his post-1997 writings (that is, after retirement from the ESA), Virilio typically adopts the language of technology and topography, events, politics, strategy, and deception in place of 'the oblique function' or discussions concerning the theories and practices of Architecture Principe (see Virilio and Petit 1999; Virilio 2000a, 2000b, 2000d). While the following chapters are organized around Virilio's important architectural ideas, to overlook the aesthetic, political, and urban contexts of their production would be to overlook the very spirit in which that research was carried out. Many of these ideas – and many of the political and aesthetic publications examined in this book – were made possible by Virilio's work in different areas: the accident, art, perception (see Virilio 2003a, 2007a, 2007b; Virilio and Lotringer 2005). For example, *The University of Disaster* (Virilio 2010b) and *Native Land: Stop Eject* (Virilio and Depardon 2008), *Grey Ecology* (Virilio 2009b), *The Futurism of the Instant: Stop–Eject* (Virilio 2010a), *The Great Accelerator* (Virilio 2012), and *The Administration of Fear* (Virilio and Richard 2012) were all written after the turn of the millennium. However, these texts do not, as a rule, focus on what might be called pure architecture – or even architecture at all, in some cases. In what follows we will be mostly concerned with the *architectural* work of Virilio rather than with the individual 'critic of the art of technology' (see Armitage 2012: 122–7).

Virilio's publications more and more favour the provisionality and contemporaneity of the interview over the permanence of the book, and the real presence of discursive work to the virtual presence and prestige of the single-authored text (Armitage 2001; Virilio and Armitage 2009, 2011; Virilio and Baj 2003; Virilio and Brausch 2011; Virilio and Lotringer 2002, 2005, 2008; Virilio and Richard 2012). It is perhaps no coincidence that, to date, Virilio has not so much resisted as shown little interest in the production of two comprehensive Readers of his work (Der Derian 1998; Redhead 2004) or prospective anthologies of his writings (Virilio 2000b, 2000d, 2002a, 2002b, 2012; Virilio and Parent 1997a). Such texts would force upon his architectural thinking, he believes, a fabricated unity and consistency. His growing preference for the interview, the short essay, and the newspaper or periodical article – as opposed to the erudite journal article or conference paper – is, debatably, a deliberate characteristic of his contemporary theorizing. It allows him continually to amend, renew, withdraw, and expound upon his architectural and other ideas and to intervene in contemporary issues and events in a way that book-length studies (which take much longer to produce) cannot.

Nevertheless, for the architecture student encountering Virilio for the first time, such vitality can bring its own set of problems. The dispersal of Virilio's architectural thinking across a wide collection of journals (some available only in French, others just difficult to obtain in any language today), along with his continuous amendment of important architectural positions, presents certain challenges to any reader who hopes to grasp Virilio's perspective on contemporary architecture or keep up with the latest changes in it. One of the key functions of *Virilio for Architects* is to organize – without uniting – the main ideas on architecture that Virilio has developed during the different phases of his career. Its aim is to trace the development of these ideas and to help students of architecture in positioning particular works within the wider architectural and intellectual, cultural, and historical contexts in which they were produced. Wherever possible, each of the next four chapters traces chronologically the various shifts in Virilio's attitude to key concepts such as 'the oblique function' or 'bunker archeology', in order to indicate what is, effectively, an unending project rather than definitive positions. To contemplate the trajectory of Virilio's career with regard to the emergence of contemporary architectural studies is not to recapture the real spirit of the French post-Second World War architectural field or to state what it should be in present-day France. Quite the reverse, it denotes what is possibly lost in conventional narratives through the reduction of this field to a sequence of famous architects and their texts, set concepts, or crucial ideas concerning the future of the city. These are all issues we shall return to in detail in Chapter 5.

CHAPTER 2

Analysing the oblique

In Virilio's view, the oblique is not a topological 'thing' we can confidently point to, like the cross on the church spire; it can only be comprehended through a defamilarized relationship with the architectural forces within which it is caught at any particular moment. This makes the oblique an extraordinarily problematic concept to define or identify. As Virilio has noted in the context of the 1960s, the term 'oblique' raises nearly as many difficulties for him as 'architecture', but when they are brought together the theoretical and practical problems can be horrendous (Virilio 1997b). The two words seem to contradict and alienate each other. Architecture is what we find in the contemporary art and science of designing and erecting vertical and horizontal buildings; the oblique is the contemporary art and science of designing and erecting slanting and sloping buildings. Virilio and Parent's Church of Sainte-Bernadette du Banlay in Nevers, France, is oblique architecture; David Childs' One World Trade Center in New York City, in the US, is vertical–horizontal architecture.

Such differences rely upon Virilio's unconventional definition of the oblique as the 'multiplication' of vertical–horizontal architecture. However, according to him, the oblique can never be simplified or clarified in terms of the binary 'additions' and 'subtractions' that are still used routinely to map out contemporary architecture – vertical versus horizontal, material versus immaterial, real space versus virtual space, and so on (Virilio and Parent 1997a).

In order to appreciate how Virilio disturbs habitual architectural additions and subtractions of this kind, we need to ascertain why Architecture Principe and 'the oblique function' became the centre of his 'third urban order' thinking in the first place. Virilio's earliest architectural research was conducted as a city planner in Paris, where he began writing on the potentialities inherent in military space. Both his chosen city and his chosen topic could hardly be further away from the oblique forms – slanting churches or sloping research centres – that became the raw materials of his later work and for which he is well known today. So what made Virilio begin to take so seriously something as seemingly uninhabitable and flowing as oblique architecture? More importantly perhaps, why should *we*? To answer these questions, the present chapter traces the development of Virilio's thinking on oblique architecture from his earliest writings in Architecture Principe's manifestos, through his and Parent's important books – *Architecture Principe 1966 and 1996* (Virilio and Parent 1997a) and *The Function of the Oblique* (Virilio and Parent 1996) – to his more radical analysis of 'the oblique' in *Bunker Archeology* (Virilio 1994a).

Post-Second World War French architecture, the École des Beaux-Arts, and Architecture Principe

Transformations taking place in post-Second World War French architecture of the 1950s and 1960s provide the single most important context for an interpretation of Virilio's early thinking on oblique architecture. Preparations for postwar reconstruction begun by the Vichy government (1940–4) and the brief success of a sober form of modernism, especially that of regionalism after the war, saw a rapid expansion and development of direct intervention exercised by the authoritarian French state in urbanism and architectural patronage (Lesnikowski 1990: 32–50). As the nation's reconstruction of its cities (Le Havre, Marseilles) and dispersal of prototypical functionalist buildings and urban forms continued apace, due to the huge commissions initiated in the 1950s known as the Grands Ensembles, modern French architects attained levels of industrialized construction unparalleled elsewhere. Indeed, construction was on a magnitude that would have been inconceivable to traditional architects before or during the war, associated as they were with the École des Beaux-Arts. This school, founded in 1671 in Paris, was not only the most important school of architecture in France but also one of the most influential such institutions in the twentieth-century world. Yet this centrality also meant that French students of architecture were among the main sufferers of the shortage of novel ideas and architectural education and of the general intellectual paralysis widespread after the war. Moreover, a meagre postwar architectural press and the consequent lack of development of a truly modern doctrinal debate also hindered the new generation of French architects.

Even so, an environment of renewed modernist orthodoxy emerged in postwar France and its former colonies of Tunisia, Morocco, and Algeria. This was a blow to traditional architects trained at the École des Beaux-Arts. It challenged their faith in the idea that Beaux-Arts trained architects would be the ones to systematize and influence French architectural style towards the creation of a post-art deco culture. Meanwhile, the 1950s saw 'Team X' – born of the rejection of the modernist ideals of artists such as Le Corbusier and others from the older generation of the Congrès International d'Architecture Moderne (1928–59) – thrive in a culture that celebrated postwar new town projects like Georges Candilis' Le Mirail in Toulouse (an expansion built in 1962 and 1964–77). However, the more formal and technological perspective of someone like, say, Jean Dubuisson, while existing beside Le Corbusier's approach, never integrated with it, while Le Corbusier himself – that nemesis of the École des Beaux-Arts – continued his housing design in the Unité d'Habitation series and forged an influential change in idiom with the chapel Notre-Dame-du-Haut at Ronchamp (1950–4).

It was with this change in idiom – alongside Jean Prouvé's researches into a light metal architecture, Paul Bossard's exploration of industrialization, and the urban utopias of Paul Maymont and Yona Friedman – that Virilio engaged in the 1950s and 1960s, through a series of articles published in Architecture Principe on urbanism, architecture, and French 'new brutalism' – that is, buildings that used concrete, exposed at its coarsest and handled with overemphasis on chunky beams that collide ruthlessly (Banham 1966; Busbea 2007; Virilio and Parent 1997a). In these articles Virilio and the other main contributor to Architecture Principe, Claude Parent, worked to make a serious analysis of the new municipal buildings in the suburbs of Paris and in modern cities elsewhere, rather than simply repudiating the reanimation of state building policy as the traditional architects of the École des Beaux-Arts had tended to do.

Although Architecture Principe had strong links with the plastic arts movement through two of its members, the painter Michel Carrade and the sculptor

Morice Lipsi, and was eager to attract architectural support, its first incarnation in 1963 was sometimes criticized for being more of an architectural in-group than part of a larger aesthetic movement in the plastic arts. While there are grounds for such criticism, to suggest that the group represented a retreat from aesthetics into architecture is, in a sense, to miss the point. One of the main aims and contributions of Architecture Principe was to demonstrate that oblique architecture is *itself* aesthetic.

Virilio has outlined his reasons for wishing to place the analysis of architecture at the centre of his aesthetics in the 1950s and 1960s:

> **With the Architecture Principe manifesto we enter into an off-limits zone, where not only the forms and materials of construction but also the techniques of the body are called into question, thereby putting an end to the postural schema of the classical age, the static state of equilibrium that it imposed on human movement.**
>
> **(Virilio 1997b: 7)**

Virilio's prioritization of architecture was founded upon a critique of both 'horizontal' (medieval low-rise) and 'vertical' (modern high-rise) cities, which last reduced the architecture of the 1960s to 'the vertical order in Manhattan' (Virilio 1997c: vi).

'Manhattan Out'

In *Architecture Principe* essays like 'Manhattan Out' (Virilio 1997c), Virilio rejected horizontal and vertical cities and the reductive notion that architecture should succumb to the vertical order in Manhattan in order to stress architecture's potentially reinventive role in city cultures. The essay considers the implications of the 'industrial power that erected its vertical monsters' and the 'search for mobility' within American culture following the postwar boom in automobiles. The main thrust of Virilio's argument is that these symbolic transformations have not seen 'verticality' disappear, as he hoped they would; rather, verticality is an American sociocultural obsession, a new, 'logical' surpassing of verticality's own tendencies. Virilio's notion of verticality is meant to convey the idea that, 'through the launching of metallic rockets off Cape Canaveral', which implies that American architecture comes to a halt there, the US can no longer 'hide its incapacity in the field of architectural problems' (Virilio 1997c: vi):

> The old distinction between nomad and sedentary still seems valid, as if a people so deeply engaged in mechanicity from its birth and in all its activities could in the end only give birth to an architecture. A technical take-off on the vertical dominant of old Gothic art is all the USA has been able to accomplish.
>
> **(Virilio 1997c: vi)**

By emphasizing the difference between nomadic (bad) and sedentary (good), modern American mechanistic architecture (and modern architecture in general) acclimatizes people to the need for the technical take-off, constructs the vertical dominant, and positions those subject to it as the 'beneficiaries' of nothing more than outdated Gothic art. Virilio refers to this phenomenon as an 'American architecture' at its 'wit's end' (Virilio 1997c: vi) and goes on to demand 'the total re-invention of the city' through urban planning and collective resistance to the human will to conquer the planet. One possible take on American architecture is to claim that it has *already* given us a great reinvention of the city. However, this idea can be accepted only if we take for granted American vertical architecture. Virilio suggests that this premise is far from innocent. The technical take-off constructs the urban domain as a great reinvention of the city rather than as the dramatic and dire situation it really is. Its vertical dominants erode the 'profound motivations for architectural creation' and reinvention, and therefore the possibility of resistance to the ongoing 'destruction of society' (ibid.).

Virilio differs, then, crucially from the advocates of vertical cities like New York – namely through the argument that oblique architectural forms like inclined planes are not simply different from the vertical order in Manhattan, but also constitutive of 'the new plane of human consciousness', as he puts it in 'Warning' (Virilio 1997g). Moreover, the vertical order in Manhattan is uninhabitable, according to 'Manhattan Out':

> **New York, that agonizing giant with its defaults[,] is for us living proof. Lack of water, electricity, mechanicity, security and safety, segregation, economic problems, the broad picture is emblematic of urban problems in the modern world.**
>
> (Virilio 1997c: vi)

Certainly New York is symbolic of the 'impotence of the political sphere and that of the imagination', as well as of the increasingly indistinguishable character of a habitat where place, passage, pleasure, and work combine and where everything is seen as 'a single temple . . . which must house all'. The relationship between the vertical order in Manhattan and 'housing all' is indistinct for Virilio, and he calls for a 'stretch of vision and imagination never before reached' and for the repudiation of 'the research of young American architects'. To 'house all', therefore, we must turn away from the vertical order in Manhattan and towards 'sedentary Europe' (ibid.).

In short, where 'young American architects' would argue that the 'uninhabitable' vertical order in Manhattan should determine modern architectural production (habitation, housing, and so on), Virilio argues that what determines such production in Europe is 'the catastrophe that tore its cities apart during the Second World War'. If we follow this logic, we must conclude that a war-torn human consciousness is inseparable from oblique architecture; hence, unlike the 'uninhabitable' vertical order in Manhattan, oblique architecture is central to debates over war, urbanism, and the city. Vertical architectural production has real 'American' sociocultural and warlike effects: it erodes inventive architectural creativity. This explains Virilio's mantra 'Manhattan Out'. More importantly, if oblique architecture is not damaged or snuffed out by Manhattan's 'uninhabitable' vertical order, then its meaning and function can be established and developed, negotiated and reconfigured through architectural intervention. This is why Virilio sees oblique architecture as crucial to the then contemporary cultural redescription of the war-ravaged city. Yet oblique architecture is not necessarily a military instrument; it might be claimed for an urban appreciation of battle-scarred façades and 'the crypts of concrete shelters . . . the origin of all architecture' (ibid.). As it is described here, oblique architecture is not simply a military instrument used to understand battle-weary cities and exploit concrete shelters – or at least it should not be; it is also a site of potential architectural resistance. Architecture Principe, Virilio suggests, should not turn its back on the new postwar oblique forms and pretend that what is happening in New York is anything but the death throes of the vertical; Architecture Principe must enter the struggle over what the oblique means now and what it could mean in the future.

Vertical architectural production has real 'American' sociocultural and warlike effects: it erodes inventive architectural creativity.

Directly or indirectly, Virilio's early recognition of oblique architecture as a site of urban struggle underpins all of his subsequent architectural thinking. Most notably perhaps, it uncannily prefigures some of his recent writing, in the new millennium, on contemporary vertical cities and 'the ultracity' (see Chapter 4). But the more immediate consequences of Virilio's architectural thinking on oblique architecture were to materialize in a 1963–6 project: an architectural study and practice written and accomplished with Parent, whose name is sometimes translated as 'the oblique function' (the phrase I shall use; see Virilio 1997e) and occasionally in the more explicit form, 'the function of the oblique', as in the eponymous title (Virilio and Parent 1996; see also Virilio 1997e). While Virilio and Parent's central arguments are now somewhat dated, their architectural studies and practices remain among the most diverse and sustained accounts of oblique architecture ever produced – with an emphasis on the death of the vertical city and the birth of the third urban order.

'The Oblique Function'

While Architecture Principe (the group) made the case for taking oblique architecture seriously, Virilio's article 'The Oblique Function' was part of a more pragmatic attempt to bring oblique architecture into dialogue with 'human groupings', urbanization, and architectural forms (Virilio 1997e). The article draws upon Virilio's own experiences as an architect in the 1950s and 1960s, is centred on a 'process of polarization' around oblique architecture, and concludes by postulating 'the third spatial possibility of architecture' (ibid.). This is, in part, a theoretical and practical attempt to confront 'the addition of individual lodgings in the towns' and 'cellular lodgings in the apartment building' (ibid.). There is an explicit sense in this text that oblique architecture will reorient our sense of space. Yet the oblique function was a very controversial idea in the early 1960s. The French architectural critic Jacques Lucan has summarized the climate of this period neatly:

> **In 1963 Claude Parent and Paul Virilio formed the Architecture Principe group with the aim of investigating a new kind of architectural and urban order. Rejecting the two fundamental directions of Euclidian space, they proclaimed 'the end of the vertical as the axis of elevation' and 'the end of the horizontal as the permanent plane': Out With Manhattan, Out With Old Villages. In place of the right angle, they adopted 'the function of the oblique', which they believed would have the benefit of multiplying usable space. Their explication of this principle, with its accompanying ideogram, frequently provoked a smile: the crossing of horizontal and vertical results in an addition sign; the crossing of two obliques results in a multiplication sign.**
>
> **(Lucan 1996: 5)**

In its initial formulation, 'The Oblique Function' speaks critically of New York, which represents the culmination of the spatial direction of the vertical and the failure of all attempts 'to reach a new type of urban unity . . . (the English city-gardens or the satellite cities)' (Virilio 1997e). The article does not simply fly in the face of this spatial direction of the vertical; one of its most important contributions to postwar debates on architecture is its theoretical and practical attempt to move beyond the failures that underpin the spatial direction of the vertical. The concept of the oblique function operates as a kind of third spatial possibility in this text, offering an alternative position on oblique architecture, as neither completely vertical nor wholly horizontal.

What remains most impressive about Virilio's approach is that it views oblique architecture *seriously* rather than irresponsibly or in ignorance. This allows 'The Oblique Function' to move beyond earlier perspectives associated with the École des Beaux-Arts and modernist traditions to produce some of the most perceptive and penetrating analyses of vertical and horizontal architectural forms available at the time. Looking at oblique architecture on its own terms, 'The Oblique Function' refuses to use the spatial directions of the vertical and the horizontal as yardsticks that could measure its success or failure. Oblique architectural functions have special virtues of their own, but it is doubtful that these would reveal themselves in relation just to the binary horizontal–vertical. It is pointless, Virilio argues, to compare the oblique function with horizontal–vertical functions, because different kinds of architecture offer different sorts of spatialities. By registering and giving credence to the specific *directions* of different horizontalities *and* verticalities, Virilio anticipates here some of the key developments in contemporary architectural studies.

For all of its radicalism, however, 'The Oblique Function' reproduces, in practice, many of the more traditional assumptions about vertical–horizontal architecture that, in theory, it seeks to question. While Virilio challenges the notion that all of the spatial directions of the vertical and the horizontal are intrinsically successful and all of the spatial directions of oblique architecture are doomed to failure, he nevertheless insists that evaluation is important in discriminating between successful and failed architecture, be it vertical–horizontal or oblique. The struggle between what is successful and what is a failure is not a struggle *against* the modern functions of architecture, but a conflict *within* them. It is in its attempt to develop a critical method for handling these problems of evaluation within the modern functions of architecture through the phrase 'oblique function' that 'The Oblique Function' ultimately comes unstuck.

As noted, Virilio locates his notion of the oblique function between two much more conventional categories of premodern and modern architecture: horizontal architecture and vertical architecture. Horizontal architecture, according to 'The Oblique Function', considers the horizontal as a permanent plane and is characterized by closeness to or intimacy with the other elements of 'urban unity', a compulsive or 'driven' nature, and a direct relationship between this nature and the additional and subtractive aspects of human groupings. Although Virilio acknowledges the importance of horizontal architecture, he refuses to romanticize it, distancing himself from the nostalgia associated with the Beaux-Arts and medievalist–preindustrial architectural traditions. The desire to return to those forms is something that only those who did not experience the cramped and inhuman conditions of premodern life can seriously indulge. For Virilio, horizontal architecture is something that did not simply die with 'the barbarity of the industrial civilization coming of age' but lingers on, in an urbanism now driven mainly by the spatial direction of the vertical (Virilio 1997e). Refusing medievalism or preindustrial visions of the town, he declares:

> **Thus an urbanism of servitude replaced a reactive urbanism.**
>
> **As important as the elements of number and gender may be, it is now proven they are unable, alone, to gain access to a new mode of urbanization.**
>
> **If we are confronted with the imperious necessity of accepting as a historical fact the end of the vertical as an axis of elevation, the end of the horizontal as permanent plane, in favor of the oblique axis and the inclined plane which achieves all the necessary conditions for the creation of a new urban order and which in addition permit the total reinvention of architectural vocabulary.**
>
> **This toppling over must be understood for what it is: the third spatial possibility of architecture.**
>
> **(Virilio 1997e)**

As this quotation suggests, Virilio is searching for something beyond an urbanism that entails our servitude to verticality, for a new mode of oblique urbanization that he calls the 'the third spatial possibility of architecture'. Nevertheless, 'The Oblique Function' argues that it is vertical architecture that has become dominant in the postwar years. Yet vertical architecture does not emerge from horizontal architecture or from the oblique function; rather, it is a flawed yet understandably human 'aspiration', something 'represented by the sanctuary or the castle' – in other words, by urban 'social conquest' (Virilio 1997e).

Virilio is searching for something beyond an urbanism that entails our servitude to verticality, for a new mode of oblique urbanization that he calls the 'the third spatial possibility of architecture'.

The move from horizontal architecture to the oblique function involves a shift from paying heed only to additional–subtractive aspects of life in human groupings to considering the multitude and variety of the aspects of human social life, while vertical architecture involves a move towards skyscrapers – the ambition to build castles in the air.

The oblique Church of Sainte-Bernadette du Banlay, Nevers

In order to illustrate how 'The Oblique Function' and 'The Nevers Work Site' (Virilio 1997d) deploy their three key theoretical categories – horizontal, oblique, and vertical architecture – in the analysis of oblique architecture, we will now consider a practical case. From 1963 to 1966, Virilio and Parent conceived and built in concrete form the oblique Church of Sainte-Bernadette du Banlay in Nevers, central France.

The eponymous Sainte Bernadette (Marie Bernarde Soubirous) experienced childhood visions of the Virgin Mary at the Grotto of Massabielle near Lourdes in 1858 and joined the Sisters of Charity in Nevers in 1866. The oblique Church of Sainte-Bernadette du Banlay employs the vocabulary of military architectural forms, manifest in the German bunkers of Hitler's Atlantic Wall built during the Second World War. A system of permanent field fortifications erected by the Nazis following the defeat of France, between 1940 and 1944, the Atlantic Wall was more than 4,000 kilometres long and ran along the European coast of the Atlantic Ocean from Denmark to Spain. As noted in Chapter 1, without the existence of the bunkers of the Atlantic Wall or the events of the Second World War, Virilio would have never been interested in architecture. 'This', says Virilio, 'is crucial' because what fascinated him was

> to what extent a full-scale war is a totalitarian space, and to what extent
> the organization of war went beyond the organization of a front-line.
> In the Second World War the whole continent was organized for war,
> with anti-airstrike defence, with defence against landing operations
> (Atlantic Wall).

> (Virilio and Limon 2001: 52)

However, according to Parent (1996: 19), the bunker forms were a belated supplement to the plans and instituted chiefly to 'play up the drama of the exterior' of the church while 'stripping' the military vocabulary 'of its lethal functions'. The church was also Virilio and Parent's first real-world attempt to articulate the oblique function; it sought to create a vigorous spatial setting established through the positioning of inclined planes. In a refusal of horizontal and vertical architectural planes, Virilio and Parent's oblique plane of the floor induced the body to move and to attune itself to unpredictability. As a consequence, the connection between the body and the church becomes dynamic and energetic instead of still and constraining. To a degree, this exploration of the variability of the oblique appears to lead in a reverse direction from the immovable concrete heaviness of the bunker. Indeed, Parent (1996: 19) has asserted that the oblique structure and the bunker form converged merely because he and Virilio set about the project with two dissimilar sets of design ideas they wanted to examine. Yet, the amalgamation between bunker concrete and a vibrant, ruptured space does exemplify the alarming and conflicting vitalities of enormous power and uneasy deadlock typical of the Cold War era. In fact, while Second World War bunkers may have offered a vocabulary of forms for the oblique Church of Sainte-Bernadette du Banlay, Virilio has said that the building had more in common with the fallout shelter than with the military bunker (Virilio and Armitage 2001b: 175). Despite the new brutalist irregular concrete and antagonistic emptiness of the construction, the oblique Church of Sainte-Bernadette du Banlay does offer the defence and safety of a more traditional religious structure. As Parent elucidates – and as can be seen in Figures 2–7:

> The church has a menacing appearance: its opaque concrete carapace is defensive, even deliberately 'repulsive' in its relation to its surroundings, but at the same time it forms a protective enclosure for the interior, which has been conceived as a grotto, in homage to the life of the church's patron saint.
>
> (Parent 1996: 19)

Figure 2 The oblique Church of Sainte-Bernadette du Banlay, Nevers, France, 2006: west elevation.

Figure 3 The oblique Church of Sainte-Bernadette du Banlay, Nevers, France, 2006: east elevation.

Figure 4 The oblique Church of Sainte-Bernadette du Banlay, Nevers, France, 2006: south elevation.

Figure 5 The oblique Church of Sainte-Bernadette du Banlay, Nevers, France, 2006: interior view of the altar.

Figure 6 The oblique Church of Sainte-Bernadette du Banlay, Nevers, France, 2006: interior with tapestries decorating the concrete wall.

Figure 7 The oblique Church of Sainte-Bernadette du Banlay, Nevers, France, 2006: north elevation.

The oblique Church of Sainte-Bernadette du Banlay, the 'first materialization' of Virilio and Parent's joint 'theoretical research', can be compared with what Virilio describes as their 'refusal of aesthetic satisfactions due to visualization' (Virilio 1997d; Armitage and Roberts 2007). For Virilio and Parent, the aesthetic satisfactions of visualization exemplify the technical and economic nature of vertical architecture. There is no link between dwelling and place in such architecture; the vertical has robbed us of any 'dwelling-place' (Virilio 1997d: xi). Virilio and Parent are not interested in the satisfactions of visualization, since they lack any religiosity; and, were we to investigate their purposes, the aesthetic satisfactions of visualization, Virilio and Parent feel, would not be 'considered proper spiritual material'. Hence they are symbolic of a mere architectural gesture rather than representing the 'use of an unusual space' (ibid.).

In contrast, the oblique Church of Sainte-Bernadette du Banlay, through Virilio and Parent's experimentation with several theoretical elements, leads them towards a 'definition of new forms of viable space, towards the concretization of new places of habitation' (Virilio 1997d: xi–xii). Unlike the aesthetic satisfactions of visualization, the 'artistic realization' of the oblique Church of Sainte-Bernadette du Banlay signals primarily the invention of a '"usual place" where experimentation replaces contemplation, where architecture is experienced in movement and its quality' (ibid.). Focusing on corporeal displacement or the 'psychological spatialization of individuals', Virilio and Parent thus sought to enhance the human body's sensitivity to reality and to habitat through a transformed contact with and perspective on the 'ground/floor element' incorporating 'partitioning, roofing, façade, etc.' (ibid.). Completely revitalizing previous construction principles, this 'transformation, made possible by the use of the oblique', Virilio (1997d: xi) wrote, 'is imminent, for the ground is the least abstract of all elements, the most "useful", and the economy will not be able to continue to neglect it' (ibid.).

. . . the oblique Church of Sainte-Bernadette du Banlay,

through Virilio and Parent's experimentation with several

theoretical elements, leads them towards a 'definition of new

forms of viable space, towards the concretization of new places

of habitation'.

The aesthetic satisfactions of visualization and the oblique Church of
Sainte-Bernadette du Banlay are used by Virilio and Parent to note topical,
even revolutionary differences between the oblique function, with its leanings
towards horizontal architecture, and a lifeless, transparent, vertical architecture.
Yet Virilio's iconoclastic reading of these 'satisfactions' fails to address the
specific pleasures of vertical constructions or to account convincingly for their
verticality; people who exclaim at the sight of very high buildings are often
aestheticizing their contented feelings of visualization. What 'The Oblique
Function' and 'The Nevers Work Site' ultimately lack is a critical vocabulary
capable of analysing the category of the oblique altogether.

Analysing the oblique: bunker archeology

In Virilio's analysis of the oblique in *Bunker Archeology* (Virilio 1994a) and
'Bunker Archeology' (Virilio 1997a), oblique architecture appears less as
a solution (as it does in 'The Oblique Function') than as a literal site of
contestation – as the military connotations of the recurrent title suggest. On
the one hand, 'The Oblique Function' offered a descriptive account of oblique
architecture, while the oblique Church of Sainte-Bernadette du Banlay offered
a practical manifestation of it; both assume that oblique architecture has an
intrinsic value. On the other hand, the 'Bunker Archeology' texts warn against
these self-explanatory and applied approaches, in which oblique architectural
forms appear to lie outside history – as if they possessed some fixed and
unchanging meaning from their very inception. Virilio's radically revised theory
of the oblique – which views its object as a former site of military struggle
without a fixed content – is something that has evolved over the post-Second
World War period and is haunted by the work of the German Nazi architect
and convicted war criminal Albert Speer (1905–81).

While the oblique represents the earliest and most persistent subject of Virilio's
published architectural writings since the 1950s, it was not until the 1970s that
he provided a more elaborated theory of oblique architecture. This theory is
reproduced and extended across a series of apparently very different essays –
such as 'Preface' and 'The Monolith' in *Bunker Archeology* (Virilio 1994a: 9–16

and 37–48) and 'Bunker Archeology', published on its own later (Virilio 1997a). What links them all is the troubling influence of Speer's concept of 'ruin value': the idea, pioneered by Speer while planning for the 1936 Summer Olympics, that a building should be designed in such a way that, if it collapsed, it left behind aesthetically pleasing ruins, which could last indefinitely without any maintenance (Speer 2003: 89–116).

Speer believed that architecture was a key field, where struggles over ruins and their value would take place continuously. Critically engaging with Speer's position, Virilio argues that the 15,000 collapsed military bunkers built by the Nazis along the coast of Western Europe during the Second World War and known collectively as the Atlantic Wall – now oblique remnants of a formerly horizontal–vertical architecture – are contradictory aesthetic spaces, sites of continuous if ambiguous pleasure, destruction, and archeological negotiation. As the three photographs from Virilio's *Bunker Archeology* (Figures 8–10) illustrate, there is a kind of 'double stake' in this oblique architecture, a double movement of monuments vanishing and resistance to their loss of original military purpose and context. As Virilio puts it, 'these works bespeak of an unknown meaning' (Virilio 1997a: xvii; see also Beck 2011).

Speer's concept of 'ruin value' haunts all of Virilio's writings of the 1970s on the oblique architecture of the military bunkers of the Atlantic Wall. It is what allows him to move beyond the kind of common sense of historical documentation that has tended to dominate postwar debate on Speer's 'spectacular repentance' (Virilio 1994a: 55; see also Sereny 1996). In the 'Bunker Archeology' texts, Virilio expands upon some of the historical and political ways of thinking about Speer and the oblique architecture of the military bunker, helping to illustrate the pitfalls of a purely historical or political approach.

The most obvious definition or 'blueprint' of the oblique architecture of the military bunker – which is 'strangely reminiscent of Aztec temples', Virilio suggests – views it as an object whose form, implicit symbolism, imagery, and geometry is 'affirmative' (Virilio 1997a: xvii). The oblique architecture of the military bunker is the former architecture of the right angle, or what was

Figure 8 'Observation post revealed by the erosion of the dunes', from Paul Virilio's *Bunker Archeology* (1994a: 173).

Figure 9 'Tilting', from Paul Virilio's *Bunker Archeology* (1994a: 177).

Figure 10 'Disappearing', from Paul Virilio's *Bunker Archeology* (1994a: 180).

once a mass anchored in the ground. This is an understanding premised upon materiality. It is a definition that, Virilio says, ignores the geometry of erosion because it is associated with the depressed right angle, with a mass no longer anchored in the ground. It confuses the oblique architecture of the military bunker with materiality, with windows designed to light the interior, with human existence regarded as something neutral. One of the problems with this definition, Virilio argues, is that it produces an ultimately blind, apsychological view of an epoch and of humankind as founded on the physical proportions of humanity; it is incapable of seeing how human psychological faculties and habitat can 'unite with the secret possibilities of individuals' (Virilio 1997a: xviii). Such a view is incapable of explaining why, for instance, the geometry of erosion and the depressed right angles of the oblique architecture of the military bunker resist not only our understanding but also the mass of the bunker, which, no longer anchored in the ground, is centred on itself, as a seemingly independent being, capable of movement and articulation. 'This architecture floats on the surface of an earth which has lost its materiality', comments Virilio (1997a:

xvii) – which suggests that the oblique architecture of the military bunker is to be viewed neither as completely determined by the depressed right angle nor as consisting, passively and indiscriminatingly, of a series of 'beach monoliths' no longer anchored in the ground.

'This architecture floats on the surface of an earth which has lost its materiality', comments Virilio . . . which suggests that the oblique architecture of the military bunker is to be viewed neither as completely determined by the depressed right angle nor as consisting, passively and indiscriminatingly, of a series of 'beach monoliths' no longer anchored in the ground.

Opposed to this definition of the oblique architecture of the military bunker is the one sometimes offered by the 'countryside's inhabitants' (Virilio 1994a: 13). These locals argue that the military bunker cannot be read as the sudden appearance of an empty, animal-like carcass, but only as a concrete landmark of fear that evokes 'too many bad memories'. This definition identifies alternative descriptions of the military bunker with a wholly imaginary experience, uncontaminated by the reality of the German occupation – with the fantasy of waiting in the wings of the Germans' banal administrative lodgings to overthrow the Gestapo, and perhaps with favouring the German blockhouse over the French farmhouse. It associates the military bunker with the French Resistance and with opposition to the German occupation and to the actual experience and 'symbols of soldiery'. Virilio argues that this is a 'hostile' but equally unconvincing view of the architecture of the bunker, which never existed independently of the reality of the German occupation. Linking the post-Second World War rise of 'a new meaning for these landmarks aligned along the European littoral' to the rise of an oblique architecture of the military bunker, Virilio outlines how his bunker archeology – by 'seeing something else springing up' – has worked historically and geographically to reorient and transform, for the benefit of architectural meaning, not only the military bunker but also the study of the Atlantic Wall (Virilio 1994a: 13). For example, Virilio's bunker archeology has always worked to counter the antagonism between his own vision and that of his contemporaries, between his semi-religious understanding of the character of the bunker and his contemporaries' symbolic rather than archeological critique of it. This means that, while at key moments the military bunker has been opposed, resisted, and revolted against by the local countryside's inhabitants under the reality of German occupation, this same reality has made it in equal measure a site of avant-garde architectural modernization and militarized ruination.

This brings us to the crux of the matter: both definitions rely on a historical–political sensibility that characterizes the oblique architecture of the military bunker in a way that is ultimately unsustainable. How much mass exactly *does* have to be firmly anchored in the ground within an affirmative geometry before the corresponding building can or cannot be regarded as 'oblique architecture'? Does the difference between immaterial imagination and material experience depend on how much one fought against the reality of the German occupation? Where do we draw the line? Virilio's view is that we cannot, that it is necessary to analyse the oblique architecture of the military bunker as a 'space of a different historical time' (Virilio 1994a: 14). In *Bunker Archeology* he settles for a third definition of the military bunker – one that stresses that the relations defining oblique architecture are in a state of continuous tension.

According to Virilio, the oblique architecture of the military bunker does not have a fixed, intrinsic 'ruin value', or a content inscribed into it; the oblique and very real forms on Atlantic beaches become, by turns, enhanced hubs and degraded vectors of ruin value in debates over architecture. If the military bunker was once a concrete mass, it now appears as the premonition of Virilio's own movements, as a coastal yet demilitarized rendezvous point in a world of abandoned fortifications. It follows that, if the process of evaluation by which we distinguish between the French farmhouse and the German blockhouse shifts over time, so too do the contents of the oblique architecture of the military bunker.

At stake in all of this is much more than the issue of ruin value. Virilio's concern is about the futility of a descriptive account of the oblique architecture of the bunker that assumes that the cultural meaning of a given bunker can be guaranteed in advance, *either* as a sign of the neutrality of human existence (as our first definition suggested) *or* as a sign of fear on the part of the countryside's inhabitants (as our second definition suggested). This architecture is not *a* sign, either of neutrality or of fear. It is not the point at which the fight for the cultural meaning of the bunker has been won or lost, but, rather, a site of continual struggle and negotiation (Virilio 1994a: 14). For Virilio, the military bunker is multi- rather than uni-empathetic, as he demonstrates with reference to its armour-plated door opening, which welcomes him as if he were a long-awaited visitor (ibid.).

In *Bunker Archeology* Virilio offers the example of 'the empathy of mortal danger' – that potent emblem of fear whose cultural meaning was less 'that of a rendezvous, and more of combat': '"if the war were still here, this would kill me, so this architectural object is repulsive"' (Virilio 1994a: 14). Virilio's theory allows him to challenge ideas of mass related to the oblique architecture of the military bunker, notably the notion that the oblique is a wholly imaginary and pure expression of individual experience. The idea of multi-empathy suggests there are no oblique architectural forms or signs that 'belong' to a particular mass and whose cultural meaning can be guaranteed forever. Rather, the struggle between war and the architectural object depends upon success or failure in giving 'repulsive' oblique architecture a multi-empathetic accent, not as mass versus imagination but as cultural meaning*s* versus cultural meaning.

The indeterminacy with which the notion of multi-empathy invests the architecture of the bunker does not mean that, as far as the latter is concerned, every hypothesis concerning the bunker is equally valid. On the contrary, it is by analysing this architecture that the capacity to *constitute* the mass of the bunker becomes available – and also, for example, people's use of its oblique forces as mere 'protection from the wind'. This is why Virilio believes that we all have a cultural stake in this form of architecture. For him, the idea that the bunker has no inherent ruin value or warlike meaning is not a liberating conclusion to reach. If such a conclusion means that no project or struggle can encapsulate the bunker's oblique architecture for us or for our enemies, it also means that there are always positions here to be identified and fought over. To say that no certain position exists on the subject of bunker architecture is not to say that we should abandon our investment in the subject; quite the reverse, this absence is what makes it so vital to take a position on it.

As *Bunker Archeology* teaches us, the oblique, almost simulated architectural forms of the bunker are not just *things* we can descriptively disregard or embrace as if they contained from the very start some permanent and static meaning related to war or subsequent ruin value.

All of this has significant implications for how Virilio believes that we should approach – if not assault – the architecture of the military bunker. To search for what Virilio (with help from Speer) might call a permanent content inside the bunker is to offer an ahistorical, self-explanatory viewpoint on its architecture – a viewpoint that cannot engage with its aesthetic, military, visual, and empathetic implications. As *Bunker Archeology* teaches us, the oblique, almost simulated architectural forms of the bunker are not just *things* we can descriptively disregard or embrace as if they contained from the very start some permanent and static meaning related to war or subsequent ruin value. Rather, when we face the bunker, we need to periodize our feelings of lurking danger – to insert them into historical time and to identify the periods of relative serenity, when not only the fixed content of the military bunker but also the relation between oblique architecture and the sudden appearance of this object on the beach remain relatively tranquil. Then we should try to identify the defining moments, when relations were reshuffled and altered, for instance through paying attention to specific parts of the bunker. In brief, any explanatory account of the fluid content of the bunker's architecture will also need to be flexible.

If it is true, as Virilio suggests, that the oblique architecture of the military bunker is an important site at which ruin value is ascertained and disputed, then this is why he takes the military bunker so seriously. It opens up the possibility of an aesthetic, military, visual, and empathetic intervention. By revealing the disquieting relations, the conflicts between opposition and resistance to armour-plated doors and thick concrete walls that *at any given moment* govern the oblique architecture of the military bunker, Virilio hopes to shift the dispositions of 'mass' and 'movement', however conditionally. He is careful to qualify his position. Not only are the opportunities for such shifts very limited and carefully governed, given the bunker's ruined and rusted state today (which makes a 'pure' evaluation of it unfeasible), but the idea of a zero-sum game in which Virilio's model of analysis replaces others merely takes us back to the historical–political models of the oblique architecture of the military bunker that he works against. Nevertheless, one of the central strategies of Virilio's architectural thinking has prompted him to enter the struggle over the military bunker at specific moments during the post-Second World War period.

Bunker Archeology is, then, more than an attempt to pursue the architecture of the bunker as a theoretical problem; it is also part of an early attempt to struggle with questions of architectural space, movement, and the event associated with the 'cities of the beyond' (see Chapter 5). Virilio (1994a: 15) suggests that the 'crushing feeling' made military bunkers a particularly disturbing category in the mid-1970s because, as he sensed it during his tours around them, that feeling was becoming ever more acute:

> **The various volumes are too narrow for normal activity, for real corporal mobility; the whole structure weighs down on the visitor's shoulders. Like**

a slightly undersized piece of clothing hampers as much as it enclothes, the reinforced concrete and steel envelope is too tight under the arms and sets you in [a] semi-paralysis fairly close to that of illness.

(Virilio 1994a: 15–16)

Virilio's argument here is that the architecture of the bunker is something that has to be *felt* rather than described.

There is, therefore, no single, all-embracing 'theory' of the oblique in Virilio's architectural work. His views shift according to the specific historical moment he is engaging with. For instance, in the post-Second World War atmosphere of the 1950s and 1960s, Virilio argues for greater attention to be paid to the marginalized sites of the oblique function like the Atlantic Wall. Yet in the 1970s he asks whether the oblique architecture of the military bunker – now inserted into human existence as something neutral, through its sudden appearance on the beach – exposes a dubious wish for the catastrophic probabilities of the environment of military bunkers. Such changes of position are not incongruous and do not mark a fault in Virilio's architectural thinking: they are a perfect illustration of his theory (summarized above) that there is forever a double stake of bunkers disappearing and resistance to their loss of initial military function and setting within the oblique architecture of the military bunker, with no fixed position assured for all time.

This chapter has offered a broadly chronological appraisal of some of Virilio's most influential efforts to theorize oblique architecture. While Virilio tended to view oblique architecture as a thing endowed with meaning in his earlier work, since the 1970s he has written of the need to analyse this category, and the archeology of the military bunker in particular, as a 'space of a different historical time'. Within the context of this analysis, the oblique becomes a site of aesthetic, military, visual, and empathetic struggle between the sudden appearance of bunker architecture on the beach and the gradual disappearance of the same architecture at a given historical moment. The architecture of the bunker is a point at which disquieting relations are negotiated and contested rather than decided beforehand. Indeed, as we shall establish in the next chapter, for Virilio, architecture is not only a question of concrete military bunkers but also a question of the critical relationship between space, matter, and materials.

CHAPTER 3

Critical space

Chapter 2 opened with a deliberation on Virilio's earliest writing on oblique architecture, with the group and the review through which he began to undertake research into 'critical space' – that is, what he identified as the crisis in the notion of the unity of three-dimensional space (Virilio 1991). This chapter traces the important theoretical debates in critical space as they arose during the 1980s, when Virilio began his architectural investigations at the request of the French Minister of Equipment and Housing, Roger Quilliot.

Two essays by Virilio have been particularly influential on subsequent interpretations both of his research and of French conceptions of critical space: 'The Overexposed City' (Virilio 1991: 9–28) and 'Improbable Architecture' (Virilio 1991: 69–100). Together, these pieces provide an important intellectual framework within which to contextualize Virilio's architectural thinking in the rest of this book. They throw light on the early stages of Virilio's conception of critical space and on the post-Architecture Principe history of his explorations. They trace the crucial theoretical debates that Virilio both inherited and departed from – as he moved from a conception of space as something unified to a conception of space as something 'in the process of being broken up' (Virilio and Armitage 2001a: 24). They critically survey the divisions that conventionally framed understandings of space during the 1980s – and they do so in terms of what I shall call 'the real space/virtual space divide'. Lastly, they pursue the move beyond this binary division through Virilio's turn to the work of the French American mathematician Benoît B. Mandelbrot (1924–2010), the advocate of fractal geometry and the discoverer of the Mandelbrot Set in 1982.

Published in French as *L'Espace critique* in 1984 (and in English as *The Lost Dimension* in 1991), 'The Overexposed City' and 'Improbable Architecture' were written at the beginning of what would prove to be one of the most influential periods in the history of critical architectural research on space: the postmodern period (see, for example, Mallgrave and Goodman 2011: 89–158). While each essay has a different emphasis – on the idea of the mediated metropolis and on the perception of architectonic forms, respectively – they are considered here alongside each other rather than consecutively, because there are significant overlaps and repetitions between them.

On the origins of Virilio's conception of critical space

Speaking about the emergence of his conception of critical space, Virilio has said that we 'must see it as the direct outcome of me joining the École Spéciale d'Architecture [ESA in Paris], in 1968, at the formal request of the students there' (Virilio and Armitage 2001a: 24). If the establishment of Virilio's architectural analyses marks a historic–intellectual turning point in his founding of the field, Virilio has also underlined that critical space was actually initiated elsewhere, in earlier architectural movements (e.g. within Architecture Principe) and in his later editorship, in 1974, of a book series entitled *L'Espace critique*, which included Georges Perec's *Species of Space and Other Pieces* (1997), originally published by Galilée. While Virilio's previous architectural research constitutes one kind of direct outcome, what he calls his later realization – 'that the *prima materia* of the architect is not matter, bricks, stones and concrete' – establishes another: the understanding that there is a diverse range of spaces, which must be constructed before they can be built up into matter and materials (Virilio and Armitage 2001a: 24).

Virilio's critical conception of space – which contains the idea that 'space finds itself in a critical situation, just like one would speak of critical times' – regards space as being 'under threat': 'Not only matter is threatened, space too is being destroyed' (Virilio and Armitage 2001a: 24). This conception not only informed his early architectural writings; it carried the *feeling* out of which his notion of critical space emerged. Individually, the contributions of Virilio provide a basis for breaking from traditions of architectural thinking about space established in ancient and modern times and related to the three spatial dimensions of length, width, and height.

Specifically, a critical conception of space offered Virilio's investigation a less 'architectural' account – that is, one less related to matter (bricks, stones, or concrete) – than that presented within the architectural – or perhaps 'material' – tradition. As Virilio puts it in an interview, 'critical space' describes a particular way of understanding space, which expresses a certain foreboding of disaster in relation to conventional ideas of physical meanings and dimensional values, spatial situations, and times, *not only* today *but also* in the future (Virilio and Armitage 2001a: 24). Embedded within such statements is a particular, perhaps fragmented theory of space that Virilio propounds: critical space *expresses* threatened meanings and destroyed feelings. Moreover, these obliterated spatial expressions and feelings could be found as far back as the 1960s, and not just from the 1980s. Virilio's insight that 'the unity of space, which served as a basis for Le Corbusier, for the Archigram group, for all of us in a sense, is in the process of being broken up' (ibid.) has since become a leitmotif for his standpoint on contemporary spatial studies. This proposition – that contemporary space is a form that expresses 'the lost dimension' – flows from Virilio's 'foreboding' of the experience of cyberspace. William Gibson's sci-fi novel *Neuromancer* (1984), which laid claim on coining the term 'cyberspace', was published in the same year as Virilio's *The Lost Dimension* – and this proposition characterizes Virilio's work in the 1980s as being committed to 'real space', to space as an actually lived social and historical reality (Virilio and Armitage 2001a: 24; see also Lefebvre 1991 and Foucault 1986).

Virilio's insight that 'the unity of space, which served as a basis for Le Corbusier, for the Archigram group, for all of us in a sense, is in the process of being broken up' . . . has since become a leitmotif for his standpoint on contemporary spatial studies.

A commitment to real space best captures the work of Virilio, and particularly his architectural research, from the 1950s to the 1980s. Virilio's work at Architecture Principe and his first important concept, the oblique function, were undoubtedly committed to real space in their logic. The oblique function, for instance, privileges real human spatial agency – the 'vectors of fatigue (ascent) and euphoria (descent)' of the individual human body in oblique architecture – over and against the 'neutral' and directionless horizontal–vertical architecture (see especially Parent 1997a, 1997b: xi, 1997c). However, Virilio's main insight – that contemporary space is *expressive* of certain annihilated meanings and can be used to discuss the 'lost' three spatial dimensions of length, width, and height – was, along with Virilio's Christian-humanist faith in the real human spatial agency that informed it, increasingly drawn into question – not only by William Gibson, but also by other architectural scholars in the mid-1980s.

Virilio's investigations in the 1980s, then, brought a new theoretical viewpoint and energy to French architectural exploration. This turn was stimulated in the second part of the decade by the arrival of a new body of architectural theory, focused not so much on cyberspace as on 'virtual space' – a phrase often used to refer to computer-generated or simulated architectural spaces that either reproduce actual environments or invent new ones with no 'real-life' equivalent (see Mandour 2010).

While the years of the mid-1980s are often identified as marking a shift in concern from real to virtual space within architectural research, there was (then as now) no easy passage from one to the other. Virilio's *The Lost Dimension* is a ferocious critique of what he felt were the shortcomings of virtual space. The publication was part of a wider intellectual dispute in which Virilio's commitment to real space challenged the very idea of virtual space; for him, actually lived, three-dimensional spatiality had withdrawn into computer-generated spaces. However, the idea of virtual space threatens Virilio's perhaps idealized or simplified conception through its questioning of the primacy of actually lived spatiality and through its positive endorsement of simulated architectural spaces. Working in critical space in the 1980s frequently involved taking a side vis-à-vis these two theoretical paradigms, even if, as Virilio notes, 'both approaches' eventually came 'to mesh into each other' (Virilio and Armitage 2001a: 24).

'The Overexposed City'

In 'The Overexposed City' Virilio provides one of the most hard-hitting and influential accounts of the real space/virtual space divide. The value of this essay is in its refusal to endorse unthinkingly the idea of virtual space and in exposing instead the inadequacy of this position on its own. Virilio aims to show how recognition of the limitations of, and differences between, real and virtual space can offer two very different ways forward for a critical consideration of spatiality.

'The Overexposed City' begins with a detailed account of the walls of separation, sections, and internal boundaries of the contemporary city in order to identify one of the clearest points of difference between the reality of physical space and the temporality of virtual space:

> **From this moment on, continuity no longer breaks down in space, not in the physical space of urban lots . . . From here, continuity is ruptured in time, in a time that advanced technologies, and industrial redeployment incessantly arrange through a series of interruptions, such as plant closings, unemployment, [and] casual labor . . ..**
>
> **(Virilio 1991: 11)**

In short, where real space privileges the continuity of lived experience and physical spatiality as the building blocks and *agents* of sociocultural urban change, virtual space privileges the discontinuity of lived experience and physical spatiality and the rupturing or interruption in time, which are the combined sociocultural and urban effects of new information and communications technologies and industrial reorganization. Virilio's point that lived experience and physical spatiality are now technologically and industrially produced draws on one of his most influential hypotheses about virtual space as a kind of disappearance: that advanced technologies do not simply reorganize whole industries, but, rather, organize and then *disorganize* the urban environment to the point of causing the permanent decay and degradation of neighbourhoods.

Real space is, according to Virilio, profoundly interrupted by the arrival of virtual spaces on the scene. However, his essay refuses to adopt a reductive reading of the real space/virtual space divide, as if that referred to two discrete, coherent moments. Just as real space is an inadequate label for the diverse range of the work carried out by Virilio, so here, too, we might prefer to speak of virtual spaces in the plural rather than of a singular virtual space. While today we tend to encounter virtual space as a more complete, if not wholly unified, theoretical concept, it is important to remember that, at the time Virilio encountered it, virtual space was still an emerging idea and set of positions.

The interface of virtual space

'The Overexposed City' breaks down virtual space into a series of representative instances that centre on the importance of three concepts, which exemplify for Virilio the virtual spaces he encountered in his research: the boundary, the 'electronic false-day', and the surface. He further distinguishes between the boundary and the electronic false-day and associates these with the interface of virtual space and the 'new scientific definition of surface', which he associates in turn with the 'contamination' of real space by virtual space (Virilio 1991: 12–17).

The concepts of the boundary and the electronic false-day express Virilio's first encounters with virtual space during the course of his research. For him, the boundary has undergone numerous changes regarding both the façade and the neighbourhood it fronts: 'From the palisade to the screen, by way of stone ramparts, the boundary-surface has recorded innumerable perceptible and imperceptible transformations, of which the latest is probably that of the interface' (Virilio 1991: 12). At the same time, in the era of the electronic false-day, where 'once the opening of the city gates announced the alternating progression of days and nights, now we awaken to the opening of shutters and televisions' (ibid.: 14). This extension of techno-industrialism into the access systems of the everyday world of the city and its façade – its face – is termed by Virilio 'the interface of virtual space' (ibid.: 12–13).

Virilio proposes that a 'new day has been added to the astronomer's solar day, to the flickering of candles, to the electric light'; it is an 'electronic false-day, and it appears on a calendar of information "commutations" that has absolutely no relationship whatsoever to real time' (Virilio 1991: 14). A significant reason why the interface of virtual space is important for him is that it exposes the relationship between space and chronology in a way that allows him to think through the contamination of real space by time, of a space–time that is both located somewhere and passes – of a new space–time, which exposes itself instantly. A commitment to real space, Virilio points out in 'The Overexposed City', tends to neglect the category of the instant on the computer interface in favour of lived spatial experience and time periods, whereas in virtual space the instant becomes not only a central concept but also, on the computer screen, the '"support-surface" of inscription' (ibid.). In short, for Virilio, as on a cinema screen, time surfaces on the computer screen.

Virilio proposes that a 'new day has been added to the astronomer's solar day, to the flickering of candles, to the electric light'; it is an 'electronic false-day, and it appears on a calendar of information "commutations" that has absolutely no relationship whatsoever to real time'.

Thus Virilio's turn to a consideration of virtual space coincided with reflecting on the contamination of lived spatiality by instantaneous temporality. While Virilio had rejected contaminated horizontal–vertical architecture and its surfaces in the 1950s, 1960s, and 1970s (see Chapter 2), during the 1980s his work turned increasingly towards the contaminations wrought by television screens and computer interfaces; there he discovered even more contaminated spatial dimensions that, for him, had 'become inseparable from their rate of transmission' (Virilio 1991: 14). The contamination of real space by time in the form of a broken unity of place and time is partly the basis for Virilio's rejection of those theories of time explored in 'The Overexposed City', where the metropolis has 'disappeared into the . . . temporality of advanced technologies' (ibid.). Yet Virilio has never been a pure critic of the contamination of real space by time (Virilio and Armitage 2001a: 24); he prefers instead a critique of both that contamination and the concomitant rebuilding of real matter, space, and time – a critique that draws upon that contamination while always seeking to question and move beyond the critic's own forebodings of contaminations shaped by the arrival of virtual space.

If advanced technologies and access systems no longer correspond to the world of the nineteenth- and twentieth-century city and its urban figures but determine their locational and temporal meanings on their behalf, it follows for Virilio that real space is being reduced by computers to a mere timetable where the true horizontal and/or vertical city of physical gateways disappears into audiovisual protocols, audience surveillance systems, and the realm of the instant – all of which have already changed the forms of public greeting and daily reception. These important insights were carefully developed during the 1980s through Virilio's work on the contamination of real space by virtual space and on the concept of the surface.

The contamination of real space by virtual space

Virilio describes the contamination of real space by virtual space in the example of a new scientific definition of surface: 'Each surface as an interface between two environments', he writes, 'is ruled by a constant activity in the form of an exchange between the two substances [e.g. the computer screen and the 'world' it represents] placed in contact with one another' (Virilio 1991: 17). If the electronic false-day and the boundary were two of the first ideas concerning the contamination of real space by virtual space that Virilio formed during the 1980s, then this new scientific definition of surface 'demonstrates the contamination at work': the '"boundary, or limiting surface", has turned into an osmotic membrane, like a blotting pad' (ibid.). Virilio's critical readings of virtual space as a contamination of real space in texts such as 'The Overexposed City' give his architectural thinking on changes in the notion of the boundary or limiting surface a certain immediacy within his architectural research, which was working to develop a critical dialogue between the 'commutation' of virtual space and the contamination of real space.

In 'The Overexposed City' Virilio argues that the surface incorporates not only the concept of the instant, but also the idea of a commutation, a substitution, exchange, or interchange through which we experience a radical separation or alienation, a 'necessary crossing, the transit of a constant activity, the activity of incessant exchanges, the transfer between two environments and two substances' (Virilio 1991: 17). Our lived spatio-temporal experience, he argues, is now an experience of radical separation, in the sense that it takes place within and is mediated through technological commutations and immaterial boundaries – what Virilio calls 'entryways hidden in the most imperceptible entities' (ibid.). By treating the instant as part of a system of commutations founded on immaterial boundaries, Virilio stresses the instant of the television screen or computer interface and its character as 'a secret transparency, a thickness without thickness, a volume without volume, an imperceptible quantity' (ibid.). There is no true physical reality in the world of the instant, where what was once 'visibly nothing becomes something' and 'the greatest distance no longer precludes perception'. Advanced technological access systems and televisual and computerized practices mean that we *must* live our real spatio-temporal conditions in an alienated way, as the greatest geophysical expanses contract and become ever more concentrated. The instant of the interface, like the technology of the screen, works largely at the level of *everything always already being there*, offered to view in the immediacy of an instantaneous transmission. For Virilio, instantaneous transmission is most powerfully present in domestic spaces; it looks natural, but in fact it represents the transformation of our living rooms into global broadcast studios for world events in which everything is always already there.

Virilio's argument is not that there is no longer any real space–time. One of his key contributions is to reveal how the instantaneity of satellites and the window of the television screen or computer interface work by bringing to each viewer the light of another day and the 'presence' of distant places; he calls this our 'abrupt confinement', which 'brings absolutely everything precisely to that "place", that location that has no location' (Virilio 1991: 17–18). In other words, there is no real space–time that is uncontaminated by our seemingly ubiquitous access to telescoped localization, position, and live televised events where places become interchangeable at will. One of the implications is that the instantaneity of ubiquity, the rapidity of the omnipresent, becomes the very *site* of struggle rather than a spatial or temporal distance to dismiss.

At the same time, it is precisely this idea of the instantaneity of ubiquity, as a site of struggle, that Virilio seeks to elaborate upon and that, according to him, results in the scientific definition of the surface as the 'atopia of a singular interface' (Virilio 1991: 18) – a seemingly placeless and timeless realm where the physical difference between the dimensions of here and there have been destroyed. One of the main gains of having this new scientific definition of surface and of the contamination of real space by virtual space is that it permits Virilio to deliberate upon the definition of the surface and to view our experience of space and time not as spatial and temporal distance but as an effect of '*speed distance*' (ibid.) – not as a reflection of real space and time but as an alienated relation. Moreover, Virilio's ruminations on the new definition of surface also include the idea of a speed distance that eliminates the notion of physical dimension. This, of course, reduces our experience of temporal and physical measurements to the speed of virtual space. This view creates some room for an active struggle with the radical erasure that is the contamination of real space by virtual space. Thus, while Virilio's previous commitment to real space had emphasized the determining role of human spatio-temporal *closeness* and *appearance* in the physical environment, his new commitment to the contamination of real space by virtual space emphasizes the determining role of human spatio-temporal *alienation* and *disappearance* from the physical environment of the city altogether. At this point, consequently, Virilio's contemplation of the new definition of surface leads him to emphasize the determining role of the intense technological acceleration of telecommunications and of the instant. As he argues, a focus upon this definition triggers not only a meditation on the contamination of real space by virtual space, but also the examination of 'a new type of concentration: the concentration of a domiciliation without domiciles, in which property boundaries, walls and fences no longer signify the permanent physical obstacle' (Virilio 1991: 18). For Virilio, an emphasis on the scientific definition of surface must also give due weight to the systems of interruption or to the contamination of real space by virtual space and its emissions – which compromise but do not wholly deny human spatio-temporal agency in these electronic shadow zones, or the possibility of spatio-temporal intervention. As individuals, we may appear as little more than passive components within the new definition of surface; but the potential for interruption, agency, intervention, resistance, and struggle remains, even if this theme remains undeveloped in Virilio's work.

The struggle to redefine the unity of time and place in the overexposed city

The ideas outlined above led Virilio to ask an important question. If the world of the overexposed city entails the introduction of a seemingly placeless domain replete with vision technologies (surveillance cameras, cinematic images, and the like), yet without distance, hidden aspects, opacity, and proximity, then where in the realm of the television screen, computer interface, and their associated processes of disappearance does the city without gates begin? (Virilio 1991: 19). Virilio is asking a question here about the relationship between our increasingly oppressive technological environment and our urge to flee, which emerges from our attempt to regain our senses and our sense of self in an era where real space is being contaminated by virtual space and which registers the possibility of spatial escape, the impossibility of temporal escape, and the progressively instantaneous character of our contemporary and illusory 'forward flight' into technology. Instantaneous technology is important for Virilio because it is through it that the struggle to redefine the unity of time and place in the overexposed city is taking place, and in it that the traditional unity of time and place in the 'underexposed' city currently enters into direct conflict with the structural capacities of the means of mass communication. This spatio-temporal struggle is always unequal because today's instantaneous technologies – together with their modes of representation and communication, media techniques, special effects, imperceptible orders, and immaterial configurations – appear to have more of an impact than those customary architectural technologies and techniques related to shelter, measurement, knowledge, and the cultural organization of time and space. Nevertheless, the struggle is never one-sided. Instantaneous technology is concerned not merely with the destruction of conventional architectural technologies and techniques, or with established cultural modes of organizing time and space, as the new scientific definition of surface seems to imply, but also with the reconstruction of the unity of time and place in the underexposed city according to the structural logic of the mass media (Virilio 1991: 22).

Instantaneous technology is important for Virilio because it is through it that the struggle to redefine the unity of time and place in the overexposed city is taking place, and in it that the traditional unity of time and place in the 'underexposed' city currently enters into direct conflict with the structural capacities of the means of mass communication.

There are two important consequences of Virilio's theory. First, it reintroduces the significance of his struggle to maintain a sense of the materiality of constructed physical elements, walls, thresholds, and levels, all precisely located. Second, it contributes to Virilio's questioning of immateriality as a contaminator of real space – which, for him, also implies that images and messages are now associated with dislocation and instability. This point is illustrated by Virilio in 'The Overexposed City', where its first consequence is 'architectonic and urbanistic in that it organizes and constructs durable geographic and political space' and the 'second haphazardly arranges and deranges space–time, the continuum of societies' (Virilio 1991: 22). It becomes clear in this context that these instantaneous and immaterial consequences are not rigidly or randomly determined in advance and that they exhibit an unbalanced spatio-temporal specificity and a sociocultural pertinence of their own. Yet Virilio notes that the 'point' is not to 'propose a Manichaean judgment that opposes the physical to the metaphysical', but, rather, to 'attempt to catch the status of the contemporary, and particularly urban, architecture within the disconcerting concert of advanced technologies' (ibid.). Virilio thus challenges the idea that architectonics and the city are 'progressing' and 'developing', thereby exposing the limitations of architects' 'continuing to invest in internal technical equipment' when architecture itself is now 'progressively introverted, becoming a kind of machinery gallery, a museum of sciences and technologies, technologies derived from industrial *machinism*, from the transportation revolution and from so-called "conquest of space"' (ibid.).

Virilio suggests that contemporary architecture's introversion and technologization, its performance, functions, constructions, and relationships have implications for how architects engage in the struggle between the city, technology, and spatiality:

> **The development of the City as the conservatory of classical technologies has already contributed to the proliferation of architecture through its projection into every spatial direction, with the demographic concentration and the extreme vertical densification of the urban milieu, in direct opposition to the agrarian model. The advanced technologies have since continued to prolong this 'advance', through the thoughtless and all-encompassing expansion of the architectonic, especially with the rise of the means of transportation.**
>
> **(Virilio 1991: 23)**

Virilio's line of argument here is significant for how it takes account of vanguard technologies and the city, architecture, disappearance, time, information, communication, and reality and for how it reconstructs his earlier commitment to real space in order to move beyond the new scientific definition of surface. Virilio's previous commitment to real space – his privileging of human spatial agency or human temporal *activity* – offers a helpful perspective from which to problematize and critique the contamination of real space by virtual space. However, Virilio does not withdraw to his earlier position of commitment to real space; he remains convinced that the world of the overexposed city and our experience of its emptiness are now constructed through televisual and computerized practices, and he refuses to accept that experience, considering it to be just the sum total of the governing structures of instantaneous technology.

In 'The Overexposed City' Virilio ultimately reveals how both his previous commitment to real space and the paradigm of contaminated virtual space are, on their own, inadequate. His conclusion refrains from offering an easy synthesis of the existing two paradigms. Rather, Virilio proceeds by evoking the work of Benoît B. Mandelbrot, whose thought belongs neither in the camp of real space nor in that of virtual space but has important affinities with both.

Recombining the real space/virtual space divide

While chronologically Mandelbrot's work on virtual space and the new geometry of fractals came before the new scientific definition of surface (Mandelbrot in fact influenced the generation of this idea), its impact on Virilio's thought tends to be presented in reverse order. In 'The Morphological Irruption' (Virilio 1991: 53–4, 55–6, 61, 66) and in 'The Lost Dimension' (Virilio 1991: 104, 109–10, 113), Mandelbrot's ideas on the deconstruction of the concept of physical dimension and on the downfall of the unity of three-dimensional space are offered as a means of recombining rather than resolving the real space/virtual space divide, while they also expose the limitations of both kinds of space.

Mandelbrot was a French and American citizen born in Poland. As a mathematician whose fractal geometry helps us discover patterns in the irregularities of the natural world, he has the rare distinction of lending his name to an aspect of mathematics that has become almost part of daily life: the Mandelbrot Set. Mandelbrot had a farsighted, nonconformist approach. He used computer power to expound a geometry with applications in many applied subjects, which was designed to reflect the complexity of the natural world. At the beginning of his *Fractal Geometry of Nature*, Mandelbrot asks:

> **Why is geometry often described as 'cold' and 'dry'? One reason lies in its inability to describe the shape of a cloud, a mountain, a coastline, or a tree. Clouds are not spheres, mountains are not cones, coastlines are not circles, and bark is not smooth, nor does lightning travel in a straight line . . . The existence of these patterns challenges us to study those forms that Euclid leaves aside as being 'formless', to investigate the morphology of the 'amorphous'.**
>
> **(Mandelbrot 1982: 1)**

The approach that he founded helps us to explain nature as we really observe it, and hence to enlarge our way of thinking. The world we live in is not innately smooth-edged and regularly shaped, like the customary cones, circles, spheres, and straight lines of Euclid's geometry; it is rough-edged, crumpled, creased, and uneven. 'Fractals' was the name that Mandelbrot applied to uneven mathematical shapes like those in nature, with structures that are self-similar over countless scales, the same pattern being duplicated over and over. Fractal geometry presents a methodical way of approaching phenomena that look more intricate the more they are magnified, and the images it produces are themselves a source of great enchantment.

While Mandelbrot's book had an early impact on Virilio, it was in his own *Lost Dimension* that Virilio sought a systematic reading of Mandelbrot for his own work in the 1980s. Mandelbrot's ideas are difficult to decipher for those of us who lack a highly developed mathematical, visual, and geometrical sense of mapping, in part because Mandelbrot's first visualization of his Set – on 1 March 1980, at IBM's Thomas J. Watson Research Center at Yorktown Heights in upstate New York – had its roots in the higher mathematics of early twentieth-century French pioneers like Gaston Julia, Henri Poincaré, and Pierre Fatou, who explored the world of complex real and imaginary numbers (that is, entities that hover between existence and non-existence; see Verhulst 2012). One of the things that Virilio admires in Mandelbrot's writings is their usefulness for understanding the notion of physical dimension (see Virilio 1991: 53–4), and this feature springs from Mandelbrot's ability to locate his thinking within a particularly intuitive notion, which deals with relations between figures and objects. Mandelbrot's preference for a pragmatic, subjectively grounded account of distinct physical dimensions *within* instantaneous technological formations allowed Virilio to dispute our dissolution within, displacement by, and submission to the speed of virtual space. And Mandelbrot's notion of physical dimension as a *subjective* process functioning within the technological worlds of instantaneity allowed Virilio to maintain the crucial accent on real space and human spatio-temporal agency without falling into a naïve defence of a real or material space in which we are free of all of the constraints of virtual space.

Capitulation to the contamination of real space by virtual space and to the new scientific definition of surface, which is connected with instantaneous technology, thus underplays the possibility of contesting speed distance and of opposing the disappearance of physical dimensions. This is central to Virilio's questioning of the disappearance of physical dimensions, with its constant tension between the incorporation (or dissolution) of the physical object and the resistance (or non-resistance) of the observer. In turn, the tension suggests an ongoing negotiation between urban, technological, and spatial objects and their observers, rather than between the messages and optical illusions of instantaneous technology – 'things' directly imposed by the speed of the means of communication. It was through Mandelbrot that Virilio's architectural research was able to address the limitations not just of the new scientific definition of surface, but also of virtual spaces as means of extermination. As we examine Virilio's contestation of virtual space in greater detail in the next two chapters, we will find neither real nor virtual space faithfully reproduced. The way Virilio contests virtual space while putting it to use alongside the real is important here.

The sudden confusion between reception and perception,
or the transformation of matter into light

Virilio's 'The Overexposed City' and 'Improbable Architecture' by no means
offered a representative account of what was happening in French architecture
in the 1980s. Others were more interested in developing theoretical and
practical 'presidential projects' related to President Valéry Giscard d'Estaing or
President François Mitterrand – for example, to their 'desire to create a series
of important public structures in Paris that would establish a new basis for
cultural and social interaction in the city and that would also stimulate French
architecture to undertake new visionary and creative efforts', such as the Grande
Arche de la Défense by Johan von Spreckelsen or the alterations to the Louvre
Museum by I. M. Pei (see Lesnikowski 1990: 44–5). Virilio has likened these
various projects and public structures to a 'sudden confusion between the
reception of images from a film projector and the perception of architectonic
forms', an image that 'clearly indicates the importance of the transformation of
the notion of "surface" and of "face-to-face" that gives way to the appearance
of the interface' (Virilio 1991: 69). This notion of a sudden confusion between
reception and perception also registers the specifically architectural, yet
increasingly cinematic, context in which the abstract theories of materiality
and immateriality outlined above were played out and practised.

Consider matter, for example – which, from the perspective of Virilio's
architectural research, 'is no longer even what it pretends to be' (real space),
'since this matter is "light"' (virtual space) (Virilio 1991: 69). Virilio's matter-
as-light is the spatial–temporal–technological moment in which light and
emission, in instantaneous projection, result in a *reception* rather than a
perception. Spellbound by the light of the computer screen's accelerated
images, we elect to accept whatever representations are presently available
within the global data bank of the internet as opposed to choosing what to
observe in the representational world all about us in everyday life. It is a form
of matter that signals a crisis in reception–perception. Virilio suggests that the
ongoing transformation of matter into light has had a major impact on his
architectural research. Indeed, from this point on, there emerged new kinds of

questions about the nature of representation that gave his architectural work on perception and reception a new relevance to the emergent transmission of the 'architectonic form-image' in advanced contemporary cultures (Virilio 1991: 70). The emphasis Virilio places here on the relevance of his own architectural research to contemporary cultures of representation and perception underpins one of the central aims of his architectural work and its direction: to understand the creation of that 'simultaneous collective response', which 'acts as a ubiquitous eye that sees everything at once' (ibid.).

This crisis in reception–perception was, for Virilio, the first indication of the transformation of matter into light, and his architectural research became increasingly concerned with the instantaneous role of cinematic technologies and techniques during the mid-1980s. Photography, multiple superimposed images, rapid-motion and slow-motion filming, and the imposition of simultaneous reception over perception helped question both the idea of materiality – or of the material culture presented in architecture as expressive of matter, of real material space – and the historical materialist view of the masses as agents not only of meaning, dimension, time, and history, but also of spatial and sociocultural change; this view was propounded by the cultural critic Walter Benjamin (see Benjamin 1971 and Elliott 2010). The cinematic and, later, the technological revolution emphasized the need to pay greater attention to the wider sociocultural and architectural structures of conscious perception on the basis of which the masses' experience of the popular arts is constructed through the mutual permeation of art and science or virtual space. Hence theory is more than an abstract issue in Virilio's architectural research. It is useful for understanding the notion of physical dimension in relation to wider historical-material, spatio-temporal, and cinematic-technological shifts in contemporary culture. One important shift is of course the ongoing demise of quattrocento perspective, related to the growth of technological devices that allowed artists from the fifteenth century onwards to project and record a representation of the world from a particular location. As Virilio has noted more generally about the theoretical developments within his architectural research, at stake is not just a move from whole to fractal dimensions, but also a move from perception to reception (Virilio 1991: 71).

This crisis in reception–perception was, for Virilio, the first indication of the transformation of matter into light, and his architectural research became increasingly concerned with the instantaneous role of cinematic technologies and techniques during the mid-1980s.

The spatio-temporal and technological upheavals associated with the transformation of matter into light also impacted upon Virilio's research practices throughout the 1980s. It is when Benjamin repudiates architecture's vital function of sheltering, not only from inclement weather but also from glances, that Virilio moves away from his architectonics – which 'no longer operates among the registers of resistance, material and appearances' – to establish his individual research projects, which involve the detailed consideration of the new order of instantaneous technology (Virilio 1991: 71). Virilio's architectural research represents a radical and remarkable attempt to develop a theoretical *practice* concerned with questions of technology within an architectural context that is perhaps more able than Benjamin's to resist the delirium of multiple interpretations of technological reproduction that persist to this day. In 'Improbable Architecture', Virilio refers to the industrial techniques at issue here as more than the multiplication of manufactured objects or the reproduction of photographic images:

> We are witnessing the sudden multiplication of dimensions of matter. The industrialization of artistic 'beauty,' so feared by Benjamin as a consequence of darkroom technique, is doubled and intensified by the cinematic sequences of 'industrialization of (scientific) truth,' which apparently did not concern the philosopher a bit.
>
> (Virilio 1991: 72)

In 'Improbable Architecture', Virilio focuses on the contemporary home as it develops into a mere technological intersection or 'nodal point' of reception for the informational city (Virilio 1991: 72–3). This highly influential text thus critiques and develops some of the key issues first put on the agenda by Benjamin in the 1930s: the relationship between office and home, the development of tele-informatics, the decline of metropolitan sedentary behaviour, the structure of architecture. (For an exemplary extension of Virilio's critique of Benjamin, see also Virilio's discussion of the office as a screen (Virilio 1991: 73–4).)

Clearly, then, there is never a single, unified concept or subdiscipline called 'critical space' within Virilio's architectural research, but a variety of different, often divergent research projects on space and technology, instantaneity, appearance, and disappearance. Virilio was one of the first to challenge the bidimensional idea of a television screen or computer interface as a 'translation' of the three dimensions of constructed space. In fact, Virilio has not only pointed to the replacement of the volume of the home by the interface of the computer screen but also to the 'new arrangement' that 'directs the more or less distant displacement of the occupant' (Virilio 1991: 73). Yet his early recognition of this 'transmutation' placed him in a marginal theoretical position, as both a critic of growing technological confinement and a symbol of mounting resistance to it. Indeed, Virilio's marginal theoretical position contributed to his decision to renew his focus on the nodal centres of 'techno-bureaucratic society' (ibid.).

Virilio: architectural theory and practice

So far this chapter has contemplated Virilio's chief architectural and theoretical encounters during the 1980s. But what do these encounters tell us about Virilio as an architect, theorist, and practitioner?

There is no doubt that Virilio should be classified as an original theorist and practitioner of architecture. But what is specifically innovative about his approach, both in theory and in practice? To adopt one of the expressions used by him in the analysis of overexposed cities, computer interfaces, and virtual spaces, Virilio is a *critic of the art of technology* (see Chapters 4 and

5 below; see also Armitage 2012: 117–39). For him, theorizing architecture characteristically involves critiquing materials on 'contaminated' space and analysing their aesthetic dimensions or technological aspects. This is not a 'disinterested' or 'objective' gesture; such critiques never claim the vantage point of impartial 'criticism'. In Virilio's view, the only theory of architecture worth having would be one that is *inside* the text or event – not outside. The proposal is not so much about scrapping older theories in favour of more fashionable ones as it is about *recombining* them (to adopt another of Virilio's important concepts) – as we've seen, for example, in the case of real and virtual space.

Recombination, as a theoretical practice exercised in Virilio's writing, involves struggling to redefine two, or several, different frameworks – say, time and place in the overexposed city – in order to recombine them or move beyond their separate individual limits. For instance, at the centre of this chapter has been a discussion of Virilio's redefinition of his earlier architectural and theoretical suppositions about 'real space', viewed in light of his encounter with the more recent 'virtual space'. Within Virilio's writings this redefinition does not involve rejecting the former in order to proceed to the latter, but recombining the two so as to open alternative architectural, aesthetic, theoretical, and technological directions. This process of redefinition is not fixed or final; for example, Virilio moves away from discussing the real space/virtual space divide, as we will see in the later chapters. Recombination can only be achieved under a particular set of conditions – or, to adopt one last concept from Virilio, at a particular historical understanding of the idea of *the lost physical dimension*. Virilio's architectural theorizing is taken here to be concerned with the notion of a lost physical dimension, in the sense that it is always informed by, and recombined in response to, events such as the sudden confusion between perception and reception at a precise moment.

Viewed together here, the notions of the *critic of the art of technology*, *recombination*, and *the lost physical dimension* are not only significant concepts and understandings within Virilio's architectural theory; they also present a means of thinking of that theory as *architectural practice*. According to Virilio, architectural theory is only valuable when it has a practical purpose, when it is practised; he is not interested in *architectural theory* but in constantly *theorizing architecture*. This distinction between 'theory' for its own sake and 'theorizing' is vital for our awareness of the spirit of Virilio's architectural work. Virilio is not interested in an unchanging, colossal object of study called 'architectural theory'. He is interested in architectural theory as intervention, as action within the urban realm, for homeless people, for travellers, and for those 'whose lives are being destroyed by the revolution brought about by the end of salaried work, by automation, by de-localization' (Virilio and Armitage 2001a: 28–9).

According to Virilio, architectural theory is only valuable when it has a practical purpose, when it is practised; he is not interested in *architectural theory* but in constantly *theorizing architecture.*

This chapter aims to provide a pathway to the immediate contexts in which Virilio practises architectural theory, in terms of the transformation of matter into light. This pathway should not be mistaken for a rerouting, an attempt to get the architectural theory out of the way before moving on to something more pertinent. Architectural theory for Virilio is less a withdrawal into arcane languages and more an effort to bend the language of space and time in order to interrogate 'rational' knowledge – for instance, concerning the housing of destitute or homeless people (Virilio and Armitage 2001a: 28–9). However, it is not the case that Virilio has lost faith in real social space and time. Rather, he strongly believes that the question of real space and time escapes the 'rational' knowledge and theoretical approaches of architecture, and of the social sciences in particular (Armitage and Virilio 2001a: 35). Where a 'rational' interpretation would regard architectural theory as an abstraction from the reality of the street corner, Virilio sees it as providing a language through which one can dispute 'rational' notions about the reality of the city. In summary, architectural theory is essential to architectural practice rather than a rerouting from it.

Just as, for Virilio, there can be no practical or useful understanding of real space without architectural theory, he holds that there can be no architectural theory of real space without architectural practice. Virilio's *theoretical* shift from real space to virtual space (which has been discussed in this chapter) was not authorized by the theories of Mandelbrot, but by wider sociocultural developments in the mid-1980s. Furthermore, the unique nature of Virilio's research at the time suggests that any derivative account of his major ideas would not only be unoriginal but also neglectful of the very spirit in which that research was generated and practised. Such an account would take up an imitative 'Virilian' architectural position within an already existing object of theoretical study.

This chapter has offered a key architectural and intellectual framework within which to contextualize Virilio's thinking *through* Virilio's thinking as deployed in 'The Overexposed City' and 'Improbable Architecture'. It has contemplated the origins of his conception of critical space within his own research on the overexposed city, the interface of virtual space, and the contamination of real space by virtual space. It has traced the debates that Virilio both inherited and departed from as he struggled to redefine the unity of time and place in the overexposed city. Finally, it has considered Virilio's effort to recombine or move beyond what I have called the real space/virtual space divide through his critical engagement with Mandelbrot and virtual space in the 1980s. In the second half of the chapter, these abstract theoretical developments were situated within the architectural context of Virilio's research and in the historical context of the 1980s, with its sudden confusion between reception and perception or the transformation of matter into light. The chapter closed with a consideration of Virilio's architectural theory and practice, both in terms of his personal uniqueness and in terms of his approach to theorizing and practising architecture.

CHAPTER 4

The big night

Into the ultracity

After becoming the first Lieutenant General of the Paris Police, an office
that he held from 1667 to 1697, Gabriel Nicolas de La Reynie (1625–1709)
invented the city's system of street lighting in a bid to make Paris safer for its
inhabitants. Installing approximately 5,000 lanterns around the city, covering
roughly 65 miles of streets, La Reynie's Parisian lanterns were equipped with a
candle, suspended by a rope at second-floor level, and lit by residents under
the supervision of neighbourhood *commissaires*. Even though the city quickly
became one of the best-lit conurbations in Europe, the Parisian administration
constantly sought new ways to improve its lighting system. In 1703 some even
proposed the idea of lighting Paris with a single huge spotlight, comprised of
four oil lamps located on top of a central tower (Caradonna 2012: 184). The
'City of Light', as the Englishman Joseph Lister subsequently referred to Paris,
attracted widespread international media attention. Over 300 years later it also
attracted the attention of Virilio.

Four of Virilio's most influential essays published during the 1990s
and 2000s – 'The Big Night' (Virilio 2000b: 2–11), 'The Unknown Quantity'
(Virilio 2003b: 128–34), 'Tabula Rasa' (Virilio 2005a: 1–24), and 'The
Ultracity' (Virilio 2010a: 32–69) – were shaped by concern with the ongoing
transformation of the 'matter' of the city into light. While on the surface these
essays are very different texts – a study of the 'false day of technoculture', an
investigation into the accident, an analysis of urban stasis and escape from what
I shall call 'cities of light', and an examination of 'anti-ecology' and escapist
strategies in the ultracity – there are good reasons for viewing them together.
They represent different responses to a number of shared sociocultural,
economic, and architectural conditions and concerns that had become prevalent
in the 1990s in France and elsewhere. Crudely put, these texts investigate the

reasons behind what Virilio calls the rise of *the false days of technoculture* from the seventeenth century to the twenty-first. These 'false days' resulted in the construction of the first great cities of the industrial world: *the big night*. All four essays argue that such false days of technoculture have little to do with the actual activities of La Reynie, but are in fact *the unknown quantity* of a deeper set of problems and anxieties within contemporary advanced societies. The four essays situate these anxieties within a shift from a contemporary culture of *urban stasis* and fixity to one of socioeconomic and technocultural *urban escape* and of 'post-architectural' urban exodus (as I will describe it). Finally, all of the texts consider the significance of the cities of light as potential forms of *the vertical ultracity* and of putting huge masses of people into motion.

'The Big Night'

'The Big Night' focuses on the fact that the sun no longer coordinates time in the city – a point of peak anxiety, for Virilio, over the loss of the purpose of sunrise and sunset. Moreover, as the sun is gradually eliminated from our increasingly urban physiology, so, too, is our consciousness of natural light. These facts alone would appear to justify Virilio's concern with the escalation of false days of technoculture in the present period and his call for us to avoid mistaking night for day. However, 'The Big Night' reveals not only that there was no religious or rural basis for the night being exorcised (there was no such category as the 'city of light' in rural life, therefore the concept of a 'city of light' was impossible for peasants to imagine), but also that the night life of cities of light, of the false days of technoculture, was absorbing a previously seasonal diurnal life. Given that our response to cities of light is *precisely over their 'necessity'*, Virilio (2000b: 3) asks the question: what is 'necessary' about the false days of technoculture?

Virilio employs the phrase 'false day of technoculture' in 'The Big Night' in order to consider how days that once extended over the whole planet have 'been replaced by the supplementary and simulated days of screens, consoles, and other "night tables"', becoming potent metaphors of wider cultural evacuations and urban anxieties in contemporary advanced societies (Virilio 2000b: 3).

Virilio refers to this process as the 'transterritoriality of nighttime' (Virilio 2000b: 4). It is a phrase used to describe what he perceives to be the convergence of 'red light districts' and of the binding together of 'no-go areas always on the go' – their convergence not only into discrete false days of technoculture but also into a larger single anxiety: the 'absolute reversal of biological cycles, with inhabitants dozing by day, awake at night' (ibid.). In 'The Big Night', for example, Virilio charts a progression from discrete false days of technoculture around overcrowded no-go areas in the US to the larger, more systematic ethnic urban campaigns, which demand independence from 'exploitative' cities of light such as Los Angeles – as in the case of the inhabitants of the San Fernando Valley, who are considering secession. 'Transterritoriality' is used here to foreground the notion that what is at stake is not the 'nighttime' as an out-of-control, anxiety-inducing *transformation of the matter of the city into light*, but an acceleration and escalation in how those transformations are *transterritorialized* within what Virilio calls sheltered *priva-topias* that are removed from the metropolis. The process of escalation involved in the false days of technoculture explains how life at night in the cities of light is increasingly *medicalized*, not to say *pathologized*. For example, Virilio focuses on the growing use of melatonin to combat insomnia, poor sleep quality, jet lag, seasonal affective disorder, and increased ocular pressures as one of the symptoms of our contemporary maladaptation to our urban surroundings.

In 'The Big Night' Virilio pursues what we might call the development of a pathological condition in the cities of light in order to consider its implications. His argument is not that the cities of light are simply a medical construction produced by the inappropriate usage of melatonin; he insists that cities of light *do*, physiologically, confuse us as to where night ends and day begins, that they *are* a real – sociocultural and historical – transformation of the matter of the city into light. What Virilio questions, then, is the idea that cities of light such as Las Vegas should become models for one, 'ultimate, "City of Light"' of global proportions (Virilio 2000b: 5). If Las Vegas seemed to arise in America's deserts almost spontaneously at the start of the 1930s, this particular city of light, and especially its pathologies, have quite a long history of diurnal development. Not only were cities of light exported to America from France – where, as we have seen, they were in development from the 1660s – but the French development was in turn influenced by an earlier form of street lighting based on oil lamps, in use in ancient Greek and Roman civilizations. Cities of light are not simply an electrically generated pathology of a preexisting day; a city of light like Las Vegas, for example, does not make night and day equivalent through the use of melatonin so much as it electrifies and overpopulates the night and depopulates the day. Cities of light are a transterritoriality that derives a major source of its diurnal resonance from its earlier manifestations and connotations – notably Greek, Roman, and French fears about crime and urban unrest. Our contemporary maladjustment to our environs through the usage of melatonin, coupled with the pathologization of La Reynie's original 'city of light', cannot be detached from the already established criminal expressions and meanings of that pathology.

What Virilio questions . . . is the idea that cities of light such as Las Vegas should become models for one, 'ultimate, "City of Light"' of global proportions.

'The Big Night' is not merely interested in an urban or architectural account of the transterritoriality of cities of light. Even as it foregrounds the diurnal nature of the false days of technoculture lived by millions of insomniac visitors to Las Vegas every year, it stresses that these days have real material effects: increasing numbers of windowless slot-machine halls, more luxury hotels, and casinos. By focusing on the pathology of cities of light, however, Virilio is able to pose the problem of light in its most paradoxical urban form. Could it be that a sociocultural reaction to light signals a reversal of the old values of roaming around the city into the new values of internet browsing and generalized technological roaming? Is that historically and architecturally plausible? For example, the creation of ever more cities of light might be said to produce more urban dislocation, neon light-induced delocalization, and accelerated displacement. More specifically, cities of light are producing a further *implosion* of our metropolitan perception. For Virilio, this does not mean that natural light has been completely eliminated from cities of light; all it establishes is that 'freeing ourselves from natural lighting (from cosmological time)' will, as 'The Big Night' puts it, escalate and frame our resemblance to 'moles roaming in a *beam of light*' (Virilio 2000b: 7).

Like the 'moles whose view of the world does not indeed amount to much', our present-day adjustment to our environment, flawed as it is by the use of melatonin, plays a key role in the construction and escalation of blindness (Virilio 2000b: 7). Unlike the moles, though, we do not serve instinct alone and we should not be seen as a simple extension of this little cylinder-shaped mammal adapted to an underground existence. 'The Big Night' grounds its discussion of our 'location' – currently dysfunctional, due to the use of melatonin – by offering an account of how much we have ignored in the increasingly luminous era begun under modernity by La Reynie. Exploring everything from aesthetics to disappearance and moral expressions, Virilio accounts for differences in architecture in terms of our ongoing, melatonin-induced maladaptation to gradually more transparent surroundings, while noting the present significance of Mies van der Rohe's 'dizzying and necessarily brief formula: Less is more' (ibid.). Indeed, this 'modern golden rule' has 'opened us up to the paradoxical logic of a new era':

> **Less is more, from the countdown to the speed record, from cubism to nuclear disintegration, from consumerism to computer science, from aerodynamics to the anorexia of top models, from technoliberalism to the cyber, from deforestation to the great ethnic massacres.**
>
> **(Virilio 2000b: 8)**

Here Virilio develops some of the arguments presented in *The Lost Dimension*. He considers, for example, how 'less is more' results in the 'absolute paradox of a society of individuals' and in the

> **nocturnal splitting off of anational and asocial urban fringes that keep growing at the expense of the older, historic quarters – and also with the**

recent creation of priva-topias in America or the Japanese 'side by side' city projects.

(Virilio 2000b: 8)

'The Unknown Quantity': farewell to the Milky Way

The false days of technoculture, we have seen, involve the identification of the 'big night' – the great cities of the industrial world around which Virilio's sociocultural anxieties are formulated – as an unknown quantity, which can then be characterized as 'a permanent accident' (Virilio 2003b: 129). The unknown quantity is a key Virilian concept, which describes how his anxieties about the mass media and their desire to impose the spectacle of the accident on us make that accident become habitable, to the impairment of the materiality of the communal world, at an 'integral' or 'global' level. In order to render Virilio's deepest fears for a world that is now foreclosed and elucidated by mathematics or psychoanalysis, he describes such fears as 'the unknown quantity' of 'a totally discovered planetary habitat over-exposed to everyone's gaze'. As Virilio suggests in 'The Unknown Quantity', it is through such false days that contemporary technoculture seeks and finds the big night to extinguish the 'exotic' (ibid.).

The false days of technoculture are not simply the extinguishing of the exotic, however; they are also 'endotic' – inside of us. The big night is a deeply emotional '*temporal compression* of sensations', the unknown quantity of both the coming '*great confinement*' and *generalized claustrophobia* (Virilio 2003b: 129). As Virilio argues, if the fracture with the duration of huge intergalactic events – globalization, electrified street lighting, and so on – is generally seen as desirable, the global, electronic culture it is giving rise to can also be perceived as a threat to the dominant order of human societies and to astronomical unity. The emotional aspects of the unknown quantity explain why Virilio (as proof of the astronomical break that is globalization) emphasizes the 'eccentric pollution phenomenon' first indicated by the Committee for the Protection of the Night-Skies; owing to 'the degree of light pollution created by excessively powerful electric lighting, two-thirds of humanity are now deprived of true night' (ibid.). Similarly, when Virilio categorically states that, on 'the European continent, for example, half the population are [sic] no longer able to see the Milky Way', pointing to 'the desert regions of our planet' as the only ones 'still plunged into darkness' (ibid.), there is nothing outrageous about his claims. To be no longer capable of observing the Milky Way is a global accident, which works through both widespread claustrophobia and our knowledge of the coming great confinement. What can Virilio's theory of the unknown quantity bring to an understanding of the cities of light with which this chapter began? Let us consider some of his formative thinking on the false days of technoculture in terms of our loss of a component of humanity's ancient inheritance: the capacity to perceive the Milky Way and the night.

The big night is a deeply emotional '*temporal compression* of sensations', the unknown quantity of both the coming '*great confinement*' and *generalized claustrophobia.*

Reflecting on people's inability to witness the Milky Way in 2003, Virilio argues that the disappearance of the night as a constituent of humanity's historical legacy follows to some degree from humanity's increasing 'contemplation of the *screen*', which

> no longer merely replaces . . . the *written document*, the writing of history, but also . . . the stars, to the point where the *audiovisual continuum* actually supplants the substantial continuum of astronomy.

> In this 'writing of the disaster' of space–time, in which the world becomes accessible in *real time*, humanity falls victim to myopia, reduced to the sudden foreclosure of a confinement created by the time accident of instantaneous telecommunications.

> (Virilio 2003b: 130)

Virilio develops this position in 'The Unknown Quantity' (Virilio 2003b: 128–34), an essay originally written for his 2002–3 'Ce qui arrive' (English translation 'Unknown Quantity') exhibition at the *Fondation Cartier pour l'art contemporain* in Paris, which also provides an excellent, distilled introduction to the central debates of 'Tabula Rasa' and 'The Ultracity', discussed below.

'The Unknown Quantity' is an account of the relationship between the nocturnal as an element of humanity's historic tradition and the false days of technoculture in the present period. However, it continues by tracing these days back to our contemporary residency within the integral accident of globalization. Citing Abel Gance's apparent wish – and that of his subsequent cinemascope supporters – that vision be suffocated, Virilio argues that our inability to glimpse the Milky Way is paralleled by the suffocation of our way of life – that is, the way of life of a species endowed with the movement of being. His example, which signals the presence of a contemporary phase of imprisonment as a result of globalization, also allows him to insist that our incapacity to catch sight of the Milky Way is a fatal problem, which has arrived only recently, with the onset of what I shall call 'terminal history'. In other words, it is a life-threatening feature, *constitutive of* a 'process running *behind closed doors*': 'Everything is . . . already there, *déjà-vu*', and 'soon even *déjà-dit*, already said'; all that is left is 'the waiting . . . for a *catastrophic* horizon that will succeed the *geographical* horizon of the round Earth' (Virilio 2003b: 130). Virilio's extended metaphors, loaded as they are, allow him to foreground what he terms the fatal history inside the history of the 'local accident', as it gives way to the great global accident. There is no history of the global accident without that other history, of the local accident. The processes running behind closed doors, of *déjà-vu*, of *déjà-dit*, of the interminable anticipation of disaster, integrate all of the hindrances and snags that previously typified sociocultural existence. Moreover, they do so

> to the point where this 'great confinement' puts an end to banishment and exclusion, in favor . . . of causal chains, since now, 'Everything arrives without it being necessary to depart', to move towards . . . the wholly other – as in the past one moved towards the horizontal limit of a landscape.
>
> (Virilio 2003b: 130)

The spherical Earth – as well as humanity and the planet's animals and plants (additional processes running behind closed doors towards a ruinous vanishing point) – is not simply dying according to this terminal history; it is being systematically and cumulatively liquidated, just like our capacity to see the Milky Way.

Virilio goes on to argue that the vanishing of night-time as an element of humanity's past and as a birthright is achieved through the systematic denial of this terminal history; by turning what is terminal into something treatable, we install a series of dual antagonisms between 'light' and 'dark', 'speed' and 'inertia', 'terminal' and 'remediable'. Reiterating the contention of *The Lost Dimension*, Virilio argues here that the loss of nightfall as an ingredient in humanity's bygone customs works through a profound historical annihilation of the entirety of matter, a kind of terminal historical timequake, and a decisive elimination of all distance that involves the unknown quantity of our terminal history. However, on its own, our contemporary history cannot adequately account for what is distinctive about the fading of the hours of darkness as pieces of humanity's historic culture after the unexpected contracting of consecutive, serial events – which, in consequence, have become simultaneous or concurrent in the advanced countries. One of the main arguments of 'The Unknown Quantity' is that the waning of the night as a component of humanity's historic heritage is culturally and spatially, terminally, historically, and temporally specific rather than natural and universal; it is multiple but increasingly singular in its form, as spatial extension and temporal duration are destroyed. This leads Virilio to a more specific analysis of extension, duration, and the departure of the dark – this feature of humanity's ancient inheritance – in the present period. 'Everything being already there' and the 'waiting for the catastrophic horizon' are not just Virilio's metaphors for the 'disappearance of the geographical horizon'; they are also metaphors for the extermination of the matter of the Earth from the cosmos, as the local accident surrenders to the global accident of 'screens' that 'blot out the horizon' (Virilio 2003b: 130–1).

Charting our contemporary period of enclosure, fear, experiences of the limit that eliminate any exterior, and deterioration of our inherited darkness, the essay describes a terminal point after our arrival at the twenty-first century, a point that signals the ending of multiple time scales. The halting of numerous time scales, Virilio suggests, is lubricated by the extinction of the spaces of the '*local time* of geophysics', which results in our being 'faced with the light years of a purely astrophysical time' (Virilio 2003b: 131). Today, then, the disappearance of night-time as an element of humanity's past becomes apparent through our belated recognition that we have 'gathered at the *Omega* point', the end point where 'there is no longer any *other* than mankind and that there is no longer any *outside* of him' (ibid.). Virilio refers to the 'ultimate figure of philanoia': a love of madness, linking 'the knowledge accident' to humankind and identifying humanity collectively as 'affirming everything' by its 'very existence', as comprehending 'everything by understanding itself in the closed circle of knowledge'. The end point of the knowledge accident, Virilio suggests, is sparked by mad scientists' excessive love of boundless 'discovery', which only escalates the false days of technoculture.

The eradication of the nocturnal as a constituent of humanity's earliest legacy is thus becoming a much more pervasive, not to say pathological or clinically symptomatic, feature of contemporary culture. Today, for example, networked or online video games have been introduced that are specifically designed to accelerate the unforeseen shortening of successive events. The abolition of night-time is thus registered at the level of '*de-realization*' in the present period, and it reaches its pinnacle in 'an insubstantial *parallel world*, where everyone gradually adjusts to *inhabiting the accident* of an audiovisual continuum independent of the real space of one's life' (Virilio 2003b: 131–2).

According to Virilio, focusing on the real space of one's life represents more than a response to our cumulative incapacity to observe the Milky Way; it articulates a wider sense of cybernetic quarantine following the 'accomplishments' of 'progress'. This is the 'progress' of information, speed, and the rise of instantaneous globalization across the world. What Virilio calls the importance of real space to our lives is not a direct reference to the unanticipated merging of sequential events that have become simultaneous; it expresses a more pervasive, 'revolutionary' sense of 'televisual ubiquity', which intensifies the 'slightest incident' and the 'tiniest attack' in the aftermath of progress. Nevertheless, this sense of television apparently existing everywhere at the same time is largely thematized through our growing failure to perceive the Milky Way. For the nonstop looping of TV images not only takes on 'the gigantic proportions of a world conflict' but also demonstrates the results of the Omega point, the 'meteorological' consequences of televisual omnipresence, and reproduces 'the effect of the butterfly's wings in Asia that creates a hurricane in Europe' (Virilio 2003b: 132; see also Armitage 2012: 95–116). By the turn of the new millennium, as globalized society set in, local societies came to withstand the highest levels of enclosure, yet found themselves outsiders. Moreover, these local societies, replete as they were with interior responses to the general feeling of televisual ubiquitousness identified by Virilio, saw themselves as increasingly subject to the unexpected, to being branded 'deviant' and pinpointed for the sake of ensuring that global presence. Alongside this rising tide of exigency and the fading of the night, Virilio charts the shift in mood among local communities that were initially keen to participate in this societal insanity but became increasingly de-globalized and de-socialized – communities 'in which the *local* is the outside and the *global* the inside of a finished world' (Virilio 2003b: 132).

According to Virilio, focusing on the real space of one's life represents more than a response to our cumulative incapacity to observe the Milky Way; it articulates a wider sense of cybernetic quarantine following the 'accomplishments' of 'progress'.

Virilio's terminal history of the disappearance of darkness and of the false days of technoculture helps explain how developments such as La Reynie's street lighting take on such significance in the twenty-first century. It suggests that there may well be wider structural reasons why we are turning to cities of light today, for example, in response to the networking of instantaneous information and communication, or as a detrimental form of geopolitics. It also suggests why cities of light, which in the seventeenth century appeared as the site of the false days of technoculture, generate the levels of accelerated anxiety they do in our time (for example, through real time triumphing over real space, through the demise of the night, or through the spread of televisual ubiquity to all areas of the globe). The false days of technoculture become the accelerated form of the expiry of nightfall – this constituent of humanity's former traditions – because *'globalization is turning the world inside out like a glove* – from now on, the near is foreign and the exotic close at hand' (Virilio 2003b: 132). For Virilio, the transterritoriality of these days – be that foreclosure, our rising incapacity to see the Milky Way, or a concentrated image of the two – is not the 'real' source of televisual omnipresence, but, rather, a technological, spatial, and temporal symptom of deeper civilizational problems. When we, like bad prophets of fortune, try to predict, in architecture, these symptoms (e.g. cities of light) rather than the underlying conditions that give rise to them, the forecast will be, at best, the 'horizons of expectation of a three-centuries-old past that is now dead and gone'. At worst, anxious expectation will fester and deteriorate into the global accident, as the false days of technoculture escalate towards 'a complete turnabout in the orientation of humanity' (ibid.).

So, if the big night of the false days of technoculture is not the *source* of televisual ubiquity, what are the *real* problems Virilio suggests they conceal? While the phrase 'false day of technoculture' goes some way to explaining *how* the big night became such a powerful sign of our times, it does not help us to understand *why* it did. What are the actual accelerated anxieties it stands for, and what purpose or function does it serve at our given – terminal – historical moment?

In order to answer these questions, 'Tabula Rasa' and 'The Ultracity' develop a methodology previously associated with the phrase 'false day of technoculture'. This methodology is based upon what I called above the medicalized or pathological approach, which is used within Virilio's architectural theories of the global accident. Virilio values this approach because it recognizes that entities like cities of light are not just spontaneous occurrences or accelerated events but *socioculturally constructed cities*, pathologized and transterritorialized within a progressively unified time scale, for example. At the same time, Virilio argues that cities of light cannot be fully explained in terms of how we react to them and pathologize them; they have a real basis. This is where his work in the 2000s departs from his medicalized approach of the 1990s concerning false days of technoculture, by combining it with what I have called above his 'terminal historical' approach to our contemporary phase of global imprisonment in a world without the stars. According to 'Tabula Rasa' and 'The Ultracity', such false days of technoculture amount to more than the advent of terminal history. Larger historical forces need to be accounted for, including terminal historical shifts in war, urbanism, and architecture. It is this recognition that leads to Virilio's distinctive reading, in these two essays, of contemporary global relocation in terms of a move from what might be described as a culture of urban stasis and fixity to one of urban escape and exodus.

From urban stasis to urban escape

In 'Tabula Rasa' Virilio outlines three military-urban categories that underpin the need to escape, crucial in the twenty-first century:

1   *War*: the experience of migration and compulsory movement induced by global human conflict.
2   *Urban stasis*: the catastrophe of modern architecture and the 'slow motion cataclysm' (Le Corbusier) of the modern city, such as New York. Urban stasis is also used to describe the belief that, 'since September 11, 2001, the cataclysm has speeded up' (Virilio 2005a: 18).
3   *Very high buildings*: the appearance of the skyscraper, which has characterized American-style urbanization for over a century, and the very high building as a cul-de-sac in the air (on 'the high-rise syndrome', see also Sudjic 2011: 397–428).

Through these three categories Virilio seeks to demonstrate that there is a 'real basis' in war and in the contemporary experience of departure. For example, the United Nations High Commission for Refugees estimates that currently 45.2 million people – more than the population of Argentina – are forcibly displaced worldwide (UNHCR 2014). Yet, for Virilio, these people have not produced the disaster of contemporary architecture. His argument is founded on the recognition that very high buildings are a terminal historical or structural feature of the ongoing calamity of the modern-day metropolis, 'essential' to its 'smooth running' rather than something that could 'solve' the urban problems of a contemporary city like New York. In order to fend off the absolute cataclysm of the contemporary city, the continuing disaster that is the modern metropolis has no alternative, Virilio claims, but to exploit very high buildings for the benefit of a few rich property owners, influential architects, and these buildings' increasing numbers of inhabitants. Virilio understands the devastation of modern architecture as generating a pressing desire for *escape* rather than a longing for urban stasis. While war, urban stasis, and very high buildings are by no means conjured from thin air (New York is indisputably a city with a degree of urban stasis), they are also categories that Virilio associates with an extreme craving for departure. For him, the idea of urban stasis assumes that the devastation of modern architecture has been overcome, when in reality it is permanent. According to 'Tabula Rasa', the traditional conception of urban stasis is organized around a set of related concepts – progress, modernity, architectural development, rationality, urbanism, the advanced societies, and so on. Because they are organizing elements, these concepts help, literally, to cement sociocultural and inner-city stability. Moreover, they present themselves as the 'natural instincts' of property owners, architects, and very high buildings' occupants, wedded to notions of inner-city progress, but actually they signal all of these people's subordination to sociocultural models of urban fixity that are being progressively destabilized by the (not yet dominant) catastrophic architectural order of acceleration examined below.

As all of this might suggest, Virilio's reading of architectural change in the present period has its basis in war and what we might label his theory of 'exodus'. For war not only generates evacuation; it also comes to dominate, and perhaps dismantle, the modern city of the skyscraper, thereby producing a city of extremes founded not on urban fixity but on resistance to it through spontaneous urban escape. The burning need to escape from war, from urban stasis, and from very high buildings, upon which Virilio's theory of exodus is established, thus exposes how today the local is becoming the outside, the global is becoming the inside, and the values of American-style urban stasis are being visibly shattered by the contemporary culture of urban departure. Just as moles adjust to their underground existence, we too must adjust to a new existence, founded not on urban fixity but on a kind of 'postarchitectural' lifestyle of forced urban exodus – what I have elsewhere called 'temporary authoritarian zones' (Armitage 2010). Undeniably, in today's global megalopolises, there exist new frontiers, movements, and districts, which are almost forbidden lands occupied by postarchitectural groups who live in the abandoned and ruined buildings of London or even on the streets of New York City. Casualties of involuntary worldwide migration, adrift in peripheral, unruly, destabilized, jobless, and socially deregulated terrain, these groups are driven in all directions by war, terrorism, drug and human trafficking, and the slow mutation of the contemporary global city into a camp. Such temporary authoritarian zones outside the law consist of the postarchitectural lifestyles of 'suspicious elements' and the multicultural populations lately driven from war-torn urban centres, such as Damascus, Baghdad, and Kabul, where permanent autonomous metropolitan settlement now belongs to the realm of history.

Virilio's reading of architectural change in the present period has its basis in war and what we might label his theory of 'exodus'.

What Virilio's reading of the contemporary period questions is the idea that our mounting inability to observe the Milky Way, the prospect of the global accident, and the reckless strategies associated with its realization are the source of false days of technoculture or the origin of postarchitectural lifestyles founded on forced urban exodus. On the contrary, we might argue that the pathologization of false days of technoculture provides a convenient if not crucial means of *developing* and *maintaining* what I shall name 'the state of departure'. This is because such a pathologization provides the basis for the ongoing *acceleration* of the typically decelerated calamity of the modern city, in support of postarchitectural lifestyles such as those found at the Hagadera refugee camp in Kenya (with a population of 138,102), which has to date replaced several former Kenyan villages and towns. The planet's largest refugee camp, Hagadera is a postarchitectural domain of new arrivals and travel restrictions, individual registrations, and panic, a 'territory' where the term 'lifestyle' refers to a 'life' of forced displacement and fear of arrest or government crackdown, the presentation of identification papers, queuing at transit centres, and mobile phones rendered silent for lack of access to credit. With a permanently expanding population, Hagadera is not so much a village or a town as a city founded on security sweeps, where one's neighbours and children are forever bogged down in blame games, illegality, insecurity, the absence of stable shelter, and the enduring presence of rebel groups, deportees, refugees, detainees, and barbed-wire fences. Refugee camps such as Hagadera proliferate, Virilio suggests, when the state of departure enters a period of rapid, involuntary urban migration. 'Tabula Rasa' offers a carefully and terminally historicized analysis of the state of departure and its transformation in the current period. In brief, this transformation involves a turn away from the 'successful' 'state of fixity' of the post-Second World War years and towards the conditions of the present, in which we are witnessing the growth of postarchitectural city forms – like the reception centre for exiles, asylum seekers, and illegal immigrants on the Italian island of Lampedusa. Since the 2000s Lampedusa has been a main entry point for immigrants, mostly from North Africa, the Middle East, and Asia. An embryonic postarchitectural city form, the island's temporary immigrant reception centre is presently overrun with refugees. Initially constructed for a maximum capacity of 850 asylum seekers, the centre now warehouses up to 50,000 illegal immigrants, many of whom are forced to sleep outside under plastic sheeting. Since 2011, many more, mainly male immigrants have moved to Lampedusa owing to their displacement by the 'Arab Spring' rebellions in Tunisia, Libya, and Egypt. Within this context, the reasons behind our excessive response to cities of light as a result of our maladjustment to our city environments – a response that is produced by, among other things, the inappropriate usage of melatonin – start to become clear. Viewed from the angle of the collapse of the state of fixity, cities of light are not just isolated transformations of the matter of the city into light that fatally escalate our sociocultural inability to perceive the Milky Way – something that can literally be projected back onto the first real cities of the industrial world, onto the 'big night'. More accurately, they are the 'already there' of the catastrophic horizon. For Virilio, then, everything is already there, already said, in the cities of light, as if hidden in plain sight. For him, all that continues is the waiting for the fading of the Milky Way that will succeed the cities of light as the big night of Planet Earth. Certainly, cities of light themselves more and more exhibit symptoms of the forced urban exodus that is a terminal feature of contemporary society and culture. And not only that; cities of light provide a means of managing that enforced urban emigration by legitimizing and popularizing postarchitectural responses to urban exile in the US and elsewhere. 'Tent cities', for example, are frequently erected in the US, without government approval by homeless people or protesters, and with government approval by state and military organizations. Refugees, hurricane evacuees, former soldiers, and displaced people of all sorts increasingly live in shanty towns, unofficial communities, and buildings made from scrap materials – like 'Dignity Village' in Oregon or 'Olympia' in Washington, DC. Living in tent cities in the era of the false days of technoculture therefore appears to Virilio to be merely one of the principal manifestations of the exigent aspiration to flee, by means of which we are all progressively put in motion for the benefit of exodus, for measures associated with the state of departure, which lend legitimacy to an extraordinary exercise of flight. Yet the growth of tent cities in the US and elsewhere is not just the result of homelessness. For these encampments can also be viewed as a preferred alternative to the false days of shelter offered by contemporary technoculture. Why not escape the enforced perpetual motion of living on the streets? Why not refuse the 'benefits' of exodus and, rather than suffering an unending state of departure, build a community, however makeshift, off a highway, under a bridge, or in the woods? Perhaps, therefore, the inhabitants of tent cities are not only rethinking the idea of the city but also challenging the spurious legitimacy that gave impetus to their direction of flight in the first place.

The move from voluntary urban fixity to involuntary urban exodus is, Virilio suggests, partly determined by the growing meteorological effects of climate change and by the upheavals of globalization, which are at their height today. Using his own theories, Virilio exposes the compulsory urban mass departure within and around cities of light as a mainly enforced urban evacuation, built on the terminal history of the perpetual catastrophe that is the contemporary metropolis. It is, specifically, the enforced exodus of an 'advanced', 'postindustrial', yet unending disaster within the modern city, a terminal history relentlessly seeking to anchor itself, in rapidly mobilized conditions, on an extremely weak, postarchitectural socioeconomic and cultural base. What began as particular studies of cities of light in 'The Big Night' and 'The Unknown Quantity' became part of a much larger project focused on mobilization, which Virilio took up in his subsequent writings on 'Tabula Rasa'.

Crucially, Virilio's terminal historical or structural accounts of the shift in contemporary mobilization in 'The Big Night', 'The Unknown Quantity', and 'Tabula Rasa' make clear that compulsory urban exodus is not simply *a* departure; it is a site of *continuous mobilization*. It has to be *put in motion*, distributed, systematized, and achieved. Naturally, the relationship between the currently subordinated state of fixity and the emerging dominance of the state of departure is not static. Rather, it is based on the ongoing processes of the ultracity, on instantaneity, and on globalization. In the remainder of this chapter we will consider how these processes of the city of extremes are explored in 'The Ultracity'.

Into 'The Ultracity': anti-ecological and escapist strategies in the city of extremes

'The Ultracity' is a diverse essay on widespread mobilization. It is not just about putting enormous quantities of people in motion, but also about the quantitative character of contemporary sociocultural development, the 'bulk carrier revolution' that 'we are seeing today, with the energy crisis' and the 'exhaustion of stocks of all kinds exposed by ecology' (Virilio 2010a: 32–3). Virilio explains the distinctiveness of extensive mobilization in terms of the debate over war, urban stasis, and very high buildings, as outlined above.

For example, prevalent mobilization is read in relation to new levels of war, the experience of relocation, and enforced movement. Yet within Virilio's account there is a sense that general mobilization has more than a war-induced relationship to these developments. 'The Ultracity' represents a major elaboration of this view. Virilio's understanding of mandatory urban exodus as a form of continuous mobilization rather than as something static implies that the ultracity has, and *must have*, an important role to play in pervasive mobilization. However, the ultracity also modifies how we think about the city of extremes. It is not necessarily the simple result of setting vast numbers of people in movement. This anti-ecological idea of putting gigantic numbers of people in transit is just one possible way of realizing the ultracity; it is what Virilio calls a 'mutation' (Virilio 2010a: 33) – a complete mutation of the once dominant and relatively stable structures of mobilization associated with the state of fixity into the emergent structures of mobilization, dominant but unstable, associated with the state of departure. However, if, as Virilio's idea of obligatory urban exodus suggests, such structures of mobilization are never static, then it becomes necessary to identify other forms of the ultracity that are based on continuous globalization and mobilization – what Virilio calls a mutation of '"just-in-time" distribution systems that were supposed to achieve the instant globalization of profit' (ibid.). Virilio does not try to identify anti-ecological cities of extremes or associate everything else with the problems linked to instantaneity. Rather, he argues that we must try to understand how – under what global conditions – putting colossal masses of people in motion could be a way to profit from the 'war' at the heart of the city (and from the wars of movement) and to construct a whole *range* of responses. Some wars of movement create an immense automobility through the mobilization of huge numbers of people, designed to activate a new transportation revolution, and they put the mass of civilian rather than military populations in motion. Not even those wars of movement that appear repeatedly in the terminal history of exodus, banishment, then expulsion are static alternatives (ecology vs anti-ecology); they are, *potentially*, terminal levels of a 'sphere of accelerating history' used to free us from the 'tyranny of distance' and adapted to the 'auto-mobilization of a domestic individuality' (Virilio 2010a: 33). Unlike anti-ecological ultracities, which tend to work through 'recourse to some order to leave for the front' (ibid.), escapist strategies in the city of extremes are about adapting to comprehensive mobilization. Such forms of the ultracity are not necessarily going to initiate putting vast combinations of people in movement as an uncomplicated mutation; they are, *potentially*, militarized forms, not yet departed but *made continuous*. The emphasis in Virilio's work on how wars of movement and the scales of a realm of accelerating terminal history are *made continuous*, are *used to liberate us from the dictatorship of distance*, and are *adapted to the automobilization of a domestic individuality* suggests a particular form of urban cultural activity: *motorized acceleration*.

Virilio's understanding of mandatory urban exodus as a form of continuous mobilization rather than as something static implies that the ultracity has, and *must have*, an important role to play in pervasive mobilization.

If we are becoming conscious of 'the exhaustion of stocks' (Virilio 2010a: 34), it is through the adoption and adaptation of particular motorized and accelerated temporalities, levels and realms of speeding history (like the 2008 installation of the closed-circuit Large Hadron Collider in Geneva, where hyperaccelerated escape strategies are performed), and sources of energy. Today the endless relocation of vast droves of people through motorized acceleration is related to a contestation over the question of energy (say, oil) and refusal of the negative cultural values attached to inertia – metabolic and decelerated temporalities. For many people from the richest countries of the world, accustomed as they are to generalized mobilization, the energy independence of nations, with its connotations of 'vigor', 'individuality', and 'homeland', is a means of ceaselessly globalizing the central experience of speed (Duffy 2009).

While we might argue that Virilio tends to obsess over extensive mobilization, focusing on the specific sources of energy and wars of movement associated with it, 'The Ultracity' is more interested in how these sources of energy are put to use, motorized, accelerated, and translated into our need for speed in the here and now. The sources of energy associated with general mobilization do not create motorized and accelerated temporalities; it is how these sources are speeded up – their *activation* – that creates such temporalities, or a 'global mobilization' (Virilio 2010a: 35). It is through these temporalities that sources of energy are detached from their dominant meanings, associated with 'the political economy of the wealth of nations', and rearticulated in new contexts, associated with 'the principle of acceleration' (Virilio 2010a: 36). The connotations of setting vast numbers of people in movement are not embedded in the act, as people's motorized acceleration and refusal of inactivity and slow temporalities suggests. The 'given' or 'natural' use of sources of energy is motorized and accelerated through this process. 'Energy', wrote the poet William Blake in his book *The Marriage of Heaven and Hell*, 'is Eternal Delight' (Blake [1790] 2000). Yet, when cited by Virilio, Blake's pronouncement, with its apparently innocent connotations of energy, comes to mean something very different when placed in the context of the undermining and terminal history of technical progress (Virilio 2010a: 34). Of course, this process cuts both ways. Since the start of the new millennium, technical progress, generated through the refusal to conserve oil essential to the survival of nations, has been *hyper*motorized and accelerated by the 'just-in-time' oil, gas, and automobile industries. Accordingly, the depredations of motorized and accelerated temporalities associated with technical progress are now shifting towards 'the chaos of a *systemic crisis*' (ibid.).

Virilio's arguments here are clearly informed by the global financial crisis of 2007–8 and by his 'anticipation of the further undermining of all national and territorial identity', which he associates with motorized and accelerated temporalities: 'What will be promoted instead is the traceability of individuals and the chaos of the mass resettlement involved in exodus for societies that will once again be dispersed in diasporas' (Virilio 2010a: 34). How this traceability of 'the *ultracity*' is created – through motorized exurbanism and 'the not far-off colonial exodus to the *ultraworld* of a distant planet' – and what this process comes to reflect are crucial matters here (Virilio 2010a: 37). Out of the motorized and increasingly accelerated Earth taken up by our mutated technical progress, a motorized and accelerated temporality is made possible – founded on endless 'growth' and the maximum exploitation of our planet's energy reserves.

Motorized and accelerated temporalities: the mutation of technical progress

As in anti-ecological cities of extremes, in the ultracity too escapist strategies are treated as just one possible form of resettling colossal hordes of people. Virilio's account of the process is by no means dystopian, as some critics might suggest. These strategies remain processes of ongoing global mobilization rather than being developments in a continuing 'technical progress', amid the dislocation of masses of people. In no way can the strategies be said to advance technical issues – like our pressing need to recognize that, 'from now on, . . . maximum carrying capacity' surpasses the 'capacity of transport, no matter what its velocity' (Virilio 2010a: 37). In this sense, the strategies only secure a *bulk carrier* mobilization, concerned with '*extremophile survival*'. The mutation of technical progress, motorized and accelerated temporalities, and escapist strategies in the ultracity can only be used to globalize (or live through) the experience of great herds of people in transit; they cannot develop it technically or provide improvements other than in a vehicular way. Here Virilio's use of exodus combines with his notion of the crucial need to escape, as a vehicular relation to our real conditions of existence – a relation in which 'the vehicle is everything' and 'the goal of the voyage' has 'no value' (ibid.). He argues that the mutation of technical progress in the context of gigantic crowds in flight corresponds to a 'bulk carrier' rather than to a vital form of life. He notes, for example, of the very high building:

> That static vehicle of cooped-up 'above ground' elevation is also . . .
> a carrier . . . for others, in a 'procreative tourism' that is getting bigger
> all the time in exotic locations. . . . These are all so many panicky signs
> of the imminent *révolution de l'emport*, carrying us away in bulk, which
> will have been brought on by the sudden revelation of the exhaustion
> of . . . resources . . .
>
> (Virilio 2010a: 38)

Virilio thus sees pervasive mobilization as 'technically developing' our real conditions of existence in a vehicular way (that is, in a motorized manner), and through a vehicular relation to these conditions.

Very high buildings or exurbanism at altitude

Both architecturally and intellectually, 'The Ultracity' is written in the spirit of an *exaggerated intervention* and demands to be understood at this level. It arises from the feeling of indignation experienced by Virilio after the appearance of the big night, the appearance of the unknown quantity, and the continuing disappearance of the Milky Way ever since La Reynie's invention of Parisian street lighting. Although most of the text is devoted to accounting for our exaggerated reactions to these developments, the later sections of 'The Ultracity' turn to contemplating the emergent architecture of cities of light. By contextualizing these cities with the help of 'the extravagant excesses of a progressive propaganda that is more eco-systemic than truly ecological', within a globally mobilized urban sprawl that strengthens 'city densities' around hybridized 'multiple towers', Virilio forcefully returns to the issue of 'the great post-urban transhumance' of contemporary 'urban agglomerations' that was raised in 'Tabula Rasa' (Virilio 2010a: 46).

Both architecturally and intellectually, 'The Ultracity' is written in the spirit of an *exaggerated intervention* and demands to be understood at this level.

It is no accident that the ultracity becomes identical with 'the future *révolution de l'emport*, the portable revolution', at a time of motorized acceleration; it is integral to the militarized urban logic not only of our lost capacity to observe the Milky Way, but also of our exodus from the industrial cities. Simultaneously, motorized and accelerated temporalities are *responsible* for the growth of 'the *static vehicle* of the Very High Building' (Virilio 2010a: 47). For the very high building is putting an end to '*dynamic vehicles* deprived of energy . . . by the exhaustion of natural resources . . . with the elevator taking the place of the domestic automobile' (ibid.). Thus an urban system that began by slowly altering our ability to see the Milky Way has not simply placed the bulk carriers of the train and jumbo jet at the centre of this 'ecosystem of networks', as underpinnings of a structure of 'delocalization that knows absolutely no restraint'. Rather, through our deteriorating capacity to survey the Milky Way we have come to an awareness, both of our vehicles and of our cities, and the process has allowed us to develop strategies related to an ultracity founded on continuous movement. Virilio explores such movement as a double issue: both one of energy (especially the pollution wrought by vehicles) and one related to a wider 'futurist fable' of the 'static vehicle' that carries the day 'once and for all over dynamic vehicles' and 'the polar inertia of technical progress' (Virilio 2010a: 48–9) – a position signalled earlier through the idea of everything being already there. Any architectural reaction to the mutated position of the vehicle in a city such as Paris must attend both to these future-oriented issues and to their multifaceted interconnection. Cities of light, in this context, are not just a *sign* of motorized and accelerated temporalities; they might also be read as a *response* to our no longer being able to examine the Milky Way:

> At the very beginning of the third millennium, the comprehensive rejection of 'urban sprawl' has a significance that is . . . an actual reversal in metropolitan centrality, with the static vehicle of the very high tower today carrying the day . . . over the whole set of dynamic vehicles of domestic automobility, with the axiality that extended the old urban center making way for a rising axiality.
>
> (Virilio 2010a: 49)

Note how the 'rejection of "urban sprawl"' here is portrayed as a 'reversal in metropolitan centrality'. Just as our increasing inability to view the Milky Way works vertically (through our looking up), so, too, does the architecture of the cities of light. 'The Ultracity' does not offer a superficial reading of the cities of light as a kind of disappearance of the old horizontal urban centre. Moreover, Virilio's intention is not to reverse the wrongs of the static vehicle of the very high building. Rather, cities of light, he suggests, signal a kind of architectural verticality – and a future wherein the vertical condition of not being able to witness the Milky Way entails urban escape, initially through the horizontal and dynamic vehicles of domestic automobility rather than perpendicular axiality. The question of very high buildings raised in the passage above is a significant one and is linked in 'The Ultracity' to an 'exurbanism at altitude', whereby 'the static vehicle of the skyscraper' mutates into a 'dynamic vehicle, as in the architect David Fisher's project in Dubai':

> **This is composed of some eighty storeys pivoting around a 'smart' vertical axis that will allow its passenger-inhabitants to change the orientation of their apartments, and with it, the view, the way you change television stations. And it will do this through voice command.**
>
> **(Virilio 2010a: 55)**

Virilio comments that very high buildings are a project that binds their verticalized 'passenger-inhabitants' together, in a kind of statelessness of the blind, wrenching them from their roots, identity, and sociality (Virilio 2010a: 55). While this idea of very high buildings evidently carries potential for understanding cities of light, the idea nonetheless remains undeveloped in 'The Ultracity'. Very high buildings are seen as ultimately isolated and extremophile, directed as they are against horizontal axiality and consequently exploiting the above-ground under *'cooped-up high-rise exclusion'* based on 'transit corridors and very high lifts' (Virilio 2010a: 56). Virilio refuses to interpret cities of light cursorily, as progressively aerialized forms of the ultracity; he sees them as triumphing 'over the ground . . . to the benefit of a stateless humanity, doomed to the transhumance of "extremophile" vitality' (Virilio 2010a: 58). For instance, at one level, cities of light could be read as markers of a posthorizontal architectural consciousness, a vigorous refusal to remain on the ground. On the other hand, it needs to be recognized that today's stateless humanity hardly has any firm ground left to refuse as the transhumance of extremophile energies continues apace. 'The Ultracity' ultimately declines to propose answers or solutions to the continual flood of accidents and catastrophes it delineates. Cities of light are not the answer; at best, they indicate a demand for architects that should be *equal to* the structural designs whose paradoxes they inherit. While 'The Ultracity' is perhaps an initial analysis of the fate of the globalized nonplace of our tiny planet and of its basis in motorized and accelerated temporalities, the essay's evocative reading of cities of light as postgeographical, even postplanetary architectural formations is prophetic and wide-ranging. Five years after its publication in French, the prolonged era of very high buildings, which continues in the Middle East and especially in China, represents, by any measure, the *escalation* of stateless, sightless, and perpendicular forms of above-ground movement that are the vertical streets of the ultracity.

In Chapter 3 we contemplated Virilio's examination of the influence of critical space on the overexposed city of the 1980s. 'The Big Night', 'The Unknown Quantity', 'Tabula Rasa', and 'The Ultracity' expanded this analysis into a wider explanation: that of the disappearance of the Milky Way, as it emerged into awareness in the 1990s and the 2000s. All four texts adopt broadly the same methodological approach, combining medicalized or pathologized and terminal historical interpretations of contemporary global urban culture. The pathological approach permitted a reading of the first great cities of the industrialized world as the big night of the false days of technoculture; what I have called Virilio's terminal approach allowed a historical investigation of the present period in terms of movement from a culture of urban stasis or fixity to one of urban exodus or escape. An amalgamation of these two approaches disclosed that what appeared to be separate false days of technoculture involving the prospect of the global accident in the cities of light was, in reality, the unknown quantity of the same desire, deeper but continuing, for urban escape within global society. Lastly, this chapter considered Virilio's introduction of the concept of the ultracity in order to explore how widespread mobilization metamorphosed into anti-ecological and escapist strategies in the city of extremes through motorized and accelerated temporalities or through the mutation of technical progress. Exurbanism at altitude – the very high buildings paraded by the ultracity – it was proposed, does not provide a technical solution to the desire for urban escape, but a posthorizontal architectural means of globalizing it.

CHAPTER 5

Bernard Tschumi, grey ecology,

and the cities of the beyond

In 1981 – three years before the publication of Virilio's *The Lost Dimension*
– the Swiss architect Bernard Tschumi wrote his 'A Manifesto of a Different
Type' (Tschumi 1996b). The 'theme of all really contemporary architecture',
Tschumi asserted, 'will be a series of disjunctions between use, form, and
social values' (Tschumi 1996b: 190). Indeed, Tschumi outlined a shift from
an architectural culture of 'coincidence' to an architectural culture of
'non-coincidence between movement and space, man, and object', its basis
being the 'inevitable confrontation between these different terms', and thus the
production of 'effects whose consequences are often unforeseeable'. Between
1981 and 1996 (the period in which he revised his 'Manifesto'), Tschumi
therefore began to suggest 'a different reading of architecture in which space,
movement, and event are independent but situated in a new relation to one
another'. Over the same period, his different reading of architecture proposed
'that the traditional elements making up architecture' should be 'broken up and
reconstructed along other axes' (ibid.). Consequently, by the time his reworked
'Manifesto' appeared in Virilio and Parent's *Architecture Principe 1966 and 1996*
(Virilio and Parent 1997a: 190–2), Tschumi was advocating that all architecture,
instead of arising from 'functional values', should arise from desire (Tschumi
1996b: 191). Nevertheless, the central premise of Tschumi's 'Manifesto' is that
'only the relation between the three levels of space, movement, and event,
creates the architectural experience'. How do we explain this apparent disjunction
between the three levels of space, movement, and event declared by Tschumi?

Equally importantly, what response does Virilio offer to the ideas contained in
Tschumi's 'Manifesto' or in Tschumi's *The Manhattan Transcripts: Theoretical
Projects* and *Architecture and Disjunction* (Tschumi 1981, 1996a)? Unlike

Tschumi, who was concerned with 'programmatic violence' in architecture or with his own querying of the 'humanist programs of the past' (Tschumi 1996b: 191), Virilio, in my view, insists on attending to the peaceful requirements of human existence and creativity. Virilio does not think that 'negative' or 'improductive' activities are a successful approach, for example, to the erection of luxurious very high buildings. He does not believe, with Tschumi, that, with different 'readings of the spatial function', the 'definition of architecture' should 'be placed at the intersection of logic and pain, rationality and anguish, concept and pleasure' (ibid.). What Tschumi's way of architectural thinking does is to advocate the disjunctions, violent or otherwise, and the anti-humanism of contemporary critical architectural activities inclusive of the architecture of very high buildings. Yet both Tschumi and Virilio invite us to think about architecture in terms of the relation between the three levels of space, movement, and event. Their work is addressed to the introduction of space, to movement, to the event or programme as a worldwide architectural plan, to the idea 'that certain traditional elements be broken up', and to a 'decomposition' that 'allows for the manipulation of each new element following the most diverse considerations, be they narrative, formal, or conceptual' (Tschumi 1996b: 191).

In contrast to conventional accounts of architecture, which tend to concentrate on stability, it is Tschumi and Virilio's consideration of the relation between the three levels of space, movement, and event that makes their approach so productive. The dynamic relation between these levels, as opposed to inertia, is what both Tschumi and Virilio feel best characterizes their architectural achievements. This may seem an obvious point to make, given today's cybernetic spaces, speeding, and event-based culture of the internet, Google, and Facebook, where virtual locations, acceleration, and events are everything. However, it is worth noting that, when Tschumi came to prominence in the 1980s, his main architectural concern was with the inscription of human movement – a concern that, like Virilio's (see Louppe 1994), was often developed from diagrams of choreography (Tschumi 1996b: 191). Moreover, when they speak of a relation between the three levels, Tschumi and Virilio are not thinking merely of dance steps. Rather, they are thinking of inscriptions that try to 'eliminate the a priori significations that could be given to the actions of personages in order to concentrate on the effect of their movements in space', where events take place (ibid.).

'Tschumism' is a term we might coin in order to elaborate on the prevailing cultural and architectural effects associated with (but not necessarily confined to) Tschumi's involvement with space, movement, and the event. Through the 1980s, 1990s, and the first decade of the new millennium, Tschumi, much like Virilio (1990), channelled his intellectual energies into producing an ongoing critique of immobility. This commentary was first published as a series of essays in art magazines and architecture journals such as *Studio International* and *Architectural Design*, which were subsequently collected in two key volumes – *The Manhattan Transcripts* and *Architecture and Disjunction* (Tschumi 1981 and 1996a) – as well as in other books, such as Virilio's *A Landscape of Events* (Tschumi 2000). What follows is an outline of Virilio's contribution to these debates – including those on Tschumism – over three decades that he sees as marking a historic turning point in contemporary global space, movement, and eventhood.

I am not simply concerned in this final chapter with accounting for what makes Virilio's and Tschumi's architectural work so creative. Tschumi is much admired, of course, as one of today's leading architects, with offices in Paris and New York. A theorist, practitioner, and activist, Tschumi's conceptions of space, movement, and event are considered by many to be groundbreaking not only because they frequently reference literary and film cultures but also because his conceptions have been realized in innovative designs that include the Parc de la Villette in Paris, which is discussed below, and the New Acropolis Museum in Athens. My aim below, though, is to ascertain what architectural conditions have given rise to Virilio's and Tschumi's architectural efforts and what we might learn from those conditions. In spite of their similar yet divergent concentrations on space, movement, and events, Virilio and Tschumi, I argue, are not merely original architects, but also trenchant critics of the global changes that are taking place in the art of architecture and in technoculture. Tschumi and Virilio have flourished because they have grasped something of these sometimes inventive vectors, trajectories, and changes, while other architects have, for the most part, simply ignored the significance of, for example, choreography. In 1997 a potentially controversial project was launched by Virilio – less an architecture of disjunction and more an architecture of conjunction, with a number of Tschumian logics and inscriptions of space, movement, and the event – under the concept 'grey ecology' (Virilio 1997f: 58–68). Grey ecology is an attempt to build upon and move beyond Virilio's earlier critical engagement with Tschumi-like spaces, movements, and events in order to propose an alternative architectural agenda for architects that faces up to recent historic changes in matter, inscription, continuous linear volumes, and the increasingly technological trajectories and vectors of human bodies. In the second part of this last chapter we will consider Virilio's grey ecology project in conjunction with the fissures and instability of 'hypercritical space', the incoherence of 'global hypermovement', and the disjointedness of dynamic 'hyperevents' (terms explained below), which characterize the extreme activities of what Virilio calls the 'cities of the beyond' (Virilio and Armitage 2009).

Tschumism

Part of Virilio's and Tschumi's architectural achievement resides in their ability to make us think of architecture in terms of the relation between the three levels of space, movement, and event. Certainly, and in the vein of Virilio, during the 1970s, 1980s, and 1990s, Tschumi succeeded in posing issues of materiality and location, boundaries, divisibility, and extension and answered them through the papers eventually gathered together in *Architecture and Disjunction*. In 'Questions of Space', for instance, Tschumi (1996a: 53–62) presents a series of 65 questions, including: 'Is space a material thing in which all material things are to be located?'; 'If space is a material thing, does it have boundaries?'; 'As every finite extent of space is infinitely divisible (since every space can contain smaller spaces), can an infinite collection of spaces then form a finite space?'; and, 'In any case, if space is an extension of matter, can one part of space be distinguished from another?' In these early articles, therefore, Tschumi persistently attempts to solve his own questions through a focus on architecture as a disjunctive space of action and eventhood. 'As a whole', he writes in the 'Introduction' to *Architecture and Disjunction*, 'these texts reiterate that architecture is never autonomous, never pure form, and, similarly, that architecture is not a matter of style and cannot be reduced to a language' (Tschumi 1996a: 3). In pure architectural terms, this volume resists 'an overrated notion of architectural form'. It aspires instead to 'reinstate the term *function* and, more particularly, to reinscribe the movement of bodies in space, together with the actions and events that take place within the social and political realm of architecture' (Tschumi 1996a: 3–4). Situated far away from 'the simplistic relation by which form follows function, or use', the book is by no means a socioeconomic tract; through contrast and argument, the texts it contains suggest that, 'in contemporary urban society, any cause-and-effect relationship between form, use, function, and socioeconomic structure has become both impossible and obsolete' (Tschumi 1996a: 4).

However, within the context of this particular discussion of Tschumism, to make such an argument is, perhaps, to miss the point. *Architecture and Disjunction* is not justified by Tschumi in pure architectural terms, but – like Le Corbusier's *Vers une architecture* (2008) and Robert Venturi's *Complexity and Contradiction in Architecture* (1984) – on the grounds of presenting a unique account of our architectural condition in the present period. This innovative explanation of our architectural condition is articulated through the terms of the relation between the three levels of space, movement, and event, in which 'today's disjunction between use, form, and social values' has become subject to a condition that, 'instead of being a pejorative one, is highly "architectural"' (Tschumi 1996a: 4). Tschumi thus describes architecture as 'the pleasurable and sometimes violent confrontation of spaces and activities' (ibid.). Through the terms of the relation between the three levels discussed here, Tschumi evokes detailed delineations of architectural space that permanently incorporate mutually exclusive or inconsistent terms and functions and, along with them, connotations of resistance: architectural enjoyment as an encounter with space that can interconnect with its more theoretical features. The programmatic language of interrogation within which Tschumi couches the essays in *Architecture and Disjunction* is resoundingly influential with those who seek to challenge 'the three classical tenets of beauty, solidity, and utility', because he is proposing that 'the programmatic dimension of usefulness be expanded into the notion of event' (Tschumi 1996a: 4). Before *Architecture and Disjunction*, the idea of linking violence to architecture, and thus to the productive and multifaceted associations between spaces and the events that happen within them, was rare – if not entirely unprecedented (Kenzari 2011). After *Architecture and Disjunction*, Tschumi's conceptions of space and programme became related to 'an architectural practice that tried to expand these concepts in the form of actual buildings' or into 'a new, dynamic, conception of architecture' (Tschumi 1996a: 5).

After *Architecture and Disjunction*, Tschumi's conceptions of space and programme became related to 'an architectural practice that tried to expand these concepts in the form of actual buildings' or into 'a new, dynamic, conception of architecture'.

Tschumi refuses the heartening view that the focus of his investigations emerged suddenly. In fact, his studies were inspired by the *événements* of May 1968 in Paris. Above all, they were stimulated by the support of other architects – those like Virilio, with whom Tschumi had demonstrated on the streets against the French state, and who were 'concerned with the need for an architecture that might change society' and 'have a political or social effect' (Tschumi 1996a: 5). In his 'Foreword' to Virilio's *A Landscape of Events*, Tschumi discusses Virilio's succession of articles composed between 1984 and 1996, revealing that 'P.V., or Paul Virilio, establishes the P.V., the *procès-verbal* of our contemporary society' (Tschumi 2000: viii). How does Tschumi manage to negotiate the 'P.V.' (as it is referred to informally in French) so as to navigate Virilio's urban chronicles and journal entries, his countdown of postmodern events, his descriptions of military and civilian technologies, speed, and technocultural change? Is it simply an extreme case of the accident of these initials? Virilio is not convinced by inertial methods of architectural philosophy, in which the dominant architectural culture of stasis denies not only movements in spaces where events take place, but also today's mishaps of all kinds – which range from the bombing of very high buildings to urban warfare in the Middle East. Tschumi suggests that Virilio's achievement does not lie in his capacity to produce a totalizing or convincing technique of architectural thought through which we can examine important structural and design-led alterations in contemporary society. On the contrary, what the terms of Virilio's enquiry persistently reveal to Tschumi is a stress on the essentially *deconstructive* character of contemporary temporality in relation to space.

In the same text Tschumi draws attention to the 'mediated blitzes' evident in Virilio's extant writings and to what he sees as Virilio's engagement with 'an exacerbated analysis of the acceleration of time' (Tschumi 2000: viii). Accordingly, Tschumi views Virilio's own architecture of disjunction and relation to the three levels of space, movement, and event as entirely consistent with the main strands in his own mode of architectural thought. Describing our architectural condition as one where space is increasingly overwhelmed by time, Tschumi also explains this approach to architectural theory as one that recognizes that society is becoming exclusively a function of time. Through this description Tschumi indicates the way in which Virilio's and his own vision of the future are founded upon and legitimated through the study of a 'duration', which is 'really a conjunction of simultaneities'. For example, it combines or articulates formerly commemorative discourses with temporal themes such as urgency in government. As Tschumi puts it, society's becoming wholly a function of time can be described as the attempt to speed up and eventually eliminate the idea of the long term. Such efforts, of course, reduce society to a particularly accelerated version of the hypermodern military-industrial complex by – paradoxically – deconstructing territory, political space, and enclosed walls through an equally accelerated version of a 'reaction time, which must be cybernated in order to cope with the ever-increasing acceleration of decisions' (Tschumi 2000: ix). For Tschumi, Virilio's accomplishment rests in his ability to articulate deconstructive discourses within his style of architectural thought, by which Tschumi means Virilio's aptitude for conveying fragmented, distorted, and dislocated discursive ideas within his ostensibly unpredictable and chaotic architectural philosophy. This kind of condensation and coupling of deconstructive discourses finds one of its most remarkable and fully realized expressions in what Virilio would surely agree is Tschumi's finest and most influential architectural work: the Parc de la Villette in Paris (1982–98).

Alexander Eisenschmidt's interview with Tschumi discusses the limits of architecture and its association with the city (Tschumi and Eisenschmidt 2012). In part, the interview investigates Tschumi's success in winning the international competition for the Parc de la Villette in 1982, which allowed him to try out his deconstructive ideas in constructed form. In the interview Tschumi deliberates on the project, its postponement for over four years, and its resumption in 1988, in order to describe what he sees as several of Parc de la Villette's defining characteristics.

Parc de la Villette develops deconstructive ideas on the effects of layering from a collection of Tschumi's own small drawings, where he considered the various ways in which a city can be arranged through movement. Tschumi's Parc de la Villette thus shifts away from an architecture purportedly founded on nature and towards an architecture overtly established on the city. Challenging the then predominant postmodern argument related to the historical context of the 1980s, when numerous architects sought to reinstate the atmosphere of the premodern city (see, for instance, Rowe and Koetter 1978), Tschumi proposed a modern city park. As Tschumi understands it, and as can be seen from the drawing and the photograph of Parc de la Villette below (Figures 11 and 12 respectively), the Parc is also, to some degree, an attempt to develop the concept of the point grid from Le Corbusier's 1925 Plan Voisin for Paris (see, for example, Fishman 1982: 205–12) – but at a totally different level.

Unlike the regular orthogonal grid suggested by Le Corbusier, which occupies the right bank of the Seine, Tschumi's Parc de la Villette seeks to investigate 'one of the most challenging explorations of the early twentieth-century avant-gardes, namely proposing a distinction between defining space and activating space' (Tschumi and Eisenschmidt 2012: 133). Tschumi comments for instance that here he 'wanted objects that activated space and generated

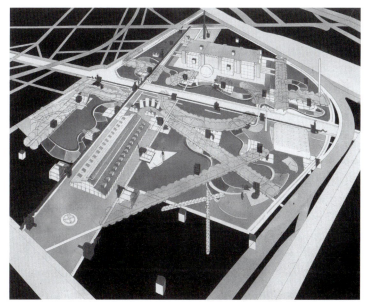

Figure 11 Bernard Tschumi, Parc de la Villette, Paris, France (1982–98).

Figure 12 Peter Mauss/Esto, Parc de la Villette, Paris, France (1982–98).

BERNARD TSCHUMI, GREY ECOLOGY, THE CITIES OF THE BEYOND

energy – almost creating fields of magnetism' (ibid.). Parc de la Villette does not mobilize architecture through its objects alone – in this context Tschumi is careful to distinguish between objects *in* space and objects that *activate* space – but through its resistance to what happens around the site.

In terms of what occurs around the Parc, for example, the organizing point grid introduces a commonality through a play on deconstructed nonprogrammatic spaces and juxtapositions, on the collision of lines (e.g. linear pedestrian paths), layers, points (e.g. the deconstructed red 'follies'), and on the fragmentation of Parc de la Villette's various museums, halls, lawns, and gardens. Tschumi's view of the relation between the three levels of space, movement, and event is not, then, simply derived from *The Manhattan Transcripts* and *Architecture and Disjunction*. Rather, his position is also developed from his attraction to the adjoining systems and strata of the city, to the intertextual positioning of disjointed architectural components, and to the ensuing events in space and the activity they generate (see, for instance, Mallgrave and Goodman 2011: 138).

The key aspects of Tschumi's influential Parc de la Villette help to explain why he regards it not as any one of all conceivable events, but as an *event that must occur under specified circumstances.*

What Tschumi takes from his own recognition of the deconstructive nature of his and Virilio's approach to architecture is that apparently stable spatial conditions have themselves become unstable and deconstructive events. Tschumi presents the idea that there is no such thing as stable spatial conditions to be (re)produced by the architect – not any more, if there ever was. While some architects may be critical of this position, regarding it as an abandonment of architectural realities and of the architect's traditional means of establishing his or her working conditions as predominantly spatial, Tschumi argues that his (and Virilio's) is less an abandonment of architectural conditions than a recognition of the end of the assumption of stable spatial conditions. As Tschumi puts it: 'In Virilio's global temporal space, landscapes become a random network of pure trajectories whose occasional collisions suggest a possible topography: here is a peak, there an abyss' (Tschumi 2000: ix).

Tschumi presents the idea that there is no such thing as stable spatial conditions to be (re)produced by the architect – not any more, if there ever was.

Tschumi's position here represents an extension of his earlier critique of architectural determinism in 'A Manifesto of a Different Type', *The Manhattan Transcripts*, and *Architecture and Disjunction* – a critique dating back to the 1980s. If architectural foundations govern the stable spatial structural design of buildings in any straightforward sense, why are architects such as Tschumi and Virilio concerned instead with instability, deconstructive events, and the acceleration of temporal reality?

Tschumi is of the opinion that architects must learn from Virilio's lessons. Tschumi's analysis of the city, of architecture, and Virilio's method of thinking architecturally about crashes, mass media, and political, public, and technocultural events represents only a part of Tschumi's project; that project is equally committed to debating the crisis in value judgements in which such analyses and methods of thinking leave architecture and, most importantly of all, what architects might do about it. Tschumi essentially presents his readers with two unambiguous options. Architects can either continue to appeal to imagined stable spatial conditions or face up to the transformations in contemporary architecture and culture and work to envisage what Virilio terms 'grey ecology' (Virilio 1997f: 57–67), in a manner alternative to that of conventional architecture but that addresses today's volatile spatial conditions.

'Grey Ecology'

The first step down the long road to a life lived within Virilio's landscape of events involves learning from both Virilio and Tschumi, while also not accepting the pollution of substances as the only form of pollution that environmentalists and ecologists should draw attention to. The essay 'Grey Ecology' is an attempt to understand contemporary forms of social space, movement, and influential events (Virilio 1997f: 58–68). This effort encompasses, for instance, the endeavour to grasp 'the sudden pollution of *distances* and lengths of time that is degrading the expanse of our habitat' (Virilio 1997f: 58). Such undertakings are not intended to persuade conventional architects to reproduce or copy Virilio's or Tschumi's logic. Rather, they are meant to convince them to recognize and respond to Virilio's grey ecology. Virilio's grey ecology project was launched in 1997, through 'Grey Ecology', the key chapter in his book *Open Sky*. *Grey Ecology* (Virilio 2009b) – a book that contains three interviews with Virilio and five critical responses by various commentators – is a collection that revises and updates Virilio's original essay. Introduced by Hubertus von Amelunxen and Drew Burk, *Grey Ecology* should not be read as a coherent 'philosophy' or as a fully formed Virilian standpoint or orthodoxy, but as a book-length interview that draws together Virilio's body of work in progress concerning the critique of the art of technology.

Virilio's grey ecology project might best be understood as an attempt to encourage traditional architects to focus on the 'pollution of *life-size* that reduces to nothing earth's scale and size' (Virilio 1997f: 58). For Virilio, this is a matter of facing up to historic shifts in nature, the nearness of human groups, and ecology in the twenty-first century. Virilio expertly develops his conception of grey ecology and explores it partly in relation to conventional architecture's reluctance to move beyond green ecology. Grey ecology, Virilio argues, is not intrinsically *opposed* to green ecology. Instead, Virilio and other architects such as Tschumi want to adopt – but also adapt – green ecology's disciplinary concerns and involvements with nature. Certainly, for Virilio, the 'artificial environment of the town' damages 'the physical proximity of beings'. Furthermore, he insists on a distinction between the quasi-natural proximity of the 'immediate neighborhood of different parts of town' and the '"mechanical" proximity of the lift, the train, or the car, and, lastly, most recently', the 'electromagnetic proximity of instantaneous telecommunications' (ibid.). To contemplate the pollution of the life-size landscape is thus not to resist green ecology or to abandon the earth, but to begin to *restore* our physical nearness and nearby communities *for* green ecology, *for* the earth. It is to present grey ecology as a complementary yet perhaps more sociable or humane ecology than the one provided by green ecology so far.

So what, precisely, does 'grey ecology' mean? Virilio's references to mechanical proximity and sociability suggest a critique of the media and call for an analysis of what he labels the '*media-staged* gap' (Virilio 1997f: 59). This is a gap or space presented by accelerated information and communications technologies, which carry only televised events or technological meanings. Consequently, Virilio conceives of the media-staged gap as a space whose technological meanings must be disarticulated from the dominant discourses of anti-green and anti-grey ecology, such as those of 'televisual intercommunication, fax, home shopping, and sex hotlines' and rearticulated in terms of green and grey ecology. Grey ecology does not have a fixed and final gap or space from which we might interpret a singular prescriptive definition of our spatial location, movement, or eventhood in the world. Meaning is not embedded in grey ecology; it is socially – even 'naturally' – produced by those who articulate and 'stage' it. If anything, grey ecology refers to a contested gap, a site of continued struggle that is neither intrinsically social nor antisocial, and lacks material – or immaterial – spatial and temporal dimensions.

However, grey ecology does not just denote a struggle over social and technological ideas of space and time; it also registers a historical change, to which those ideas are a response. This signifies that the concept of grey ecology cannot just mean anything we want it to mean. Virilio suggests that the notion registers numerous shifts in contemporary social and technological space, movement, and influential events. These shifts, I argue, are connected with the arrival of what I shall call hypercritical space, global hypermovement, and hyperhuman movement – or what I prefer to name the 'revolution of the hyperevent'.

Critical and hypercritical space

As we saw in Chapter 3, Virilio coined the phrase 'critical space' in the 1980s. It denotes more than the spatial, bodily, and mental territories wherein we locate ourselves, since, as Verena Andermatt Conley (2013: 55) writes, space 'mobilizes' not only 'many of Virilio's reflections on the condition of our world', but also his assessment that 'what Cartesian philosophy had called *res extensa* does not apply to contemporary life'. 'Determined by displacement', space is thus currently 'discernible both through and *as* movement' (ibid.). Virilio introduces space as a creation of both acceleration and inertia. His accelerated conception of space consequently allows him to express space as a vector, as the subsequent movement of an object on which numerous forces are being applied. Virilio's work on critical space draws upon his findings in *The Lost Dimension* (Virilio 1991), which demonstrate the increasing significance of technological modes and logistics of perception, according to the relationship between the transfer and radiance of the light that reveals the Earth to its inhabitant-observers. As Virilio recognizes in *Bunker Archeology* (Virilio 1994a; see Chapter 1) and elsewhere, however, critical space does not simply have implications for perception but also creates new ways of living, of considering war, and of elucidating our feeling that a transformation in lived spatial awareness has occurred since the end of the Second World War.

As the armed forces of the Axis and Allied powers intended, airborne attacks on the railways, on the highways, and on noncombatant inhabitants behind urban defences obliterated the previously ineradicable defences that had been instituted on several fronts during the First World War. Critical space is, therefore, closely associated with the emergence of new wars conducted aerially throughout the twentieth century, and particularly with the arrival of the atom bomb, which made it obvious that, from here on in, warfare would be global. More generally, from the 1980s onwards, Virilio links the sociocultural effects of critical space (for instance, on telluric spaces, human subjectivities, existential relationships, and urban environments) to the spatial production of suffering as a form of disappearance. Militarized existential and technological relations increasingly characterize, then, the connection we maintain with subjective space. In addition, ever since the offensive on civilian populations that took place in the Second World War, a logistics of acceleration has disseminated not only terror but also new states of global urban movement, as we saw in Chapter 4. In *Speed & Politics: An Essay on Dromology* (Virilio 1986), for instance,

Virilio pursues the history of acceleration as the feature that changes western conceptions of time–space coordinates – apart from accelerating people, animals, technologies, and information to a point where a new 'lost dimension' causes long-established ideas of space to enter a critical phase and become eliminated.

While Virilio's idea of critical space began in Paris in 1984, it was arguably at its most persuasive in western architectural debates between the mid-1980s and the mid-1990s. Critical space was thus associated with space becoming '(1) critical', but also '(2) a critical concept' (Andermatt Conley 2013: 56). However, as the landscape of events erupted in the 1990s, critical space as a concept seemed less and less viable to Virilio as *the* explanatory notion of the lost dimension – the politicization of space – and as *the* critical theoretical approach to questions concerning the overexposure of the city and the disappearance of all boundaries from the urban realm. Apparently, at least, Virilio's key explanatory idea of the lost dimension of critical space – namely his emphasis on automated time, on our growing dislocation, on our transmission through an ever-accelerating movement that challenges the very concept of departure, and on our transforming everything into an arrival – also turned out to be problematic. 'Critical space' was not flexible enough to handle the increasingly diverse spaces and unstable global 'places' in which we find ourselves in a 'space' deprived of place, in which the collapse of spatial landmarks and of temporal distances negates all possibilities of place.

What I term *hypercritical space* emerges out of Virilio's writings of the 1990s and is associated with the apparent decline of his interest in traditional spaces and telluric methods of spatial production (e.g. maritime spaces) and the rise of his interest in virtual and cybernetic spaces (e.g. the intense nearness of telecommunications, or supposed 'intelligent' and interconnected cities). Hypercritical space is associated with the emergence of a new space–time premised upon 'teletechnologies of action at a distance', which essentially introduce a global '*urban ecology*' (Virilio 1997f: 59). The global nature of hypercritical space is partly the product of the 'world-city' in Virilio's language. Cheaper telecommunications costs, along with the rise of 'on-the-spot tourism' and, equally importantly, the 'cocooning and interactivity' of the internet, have 'turned a world', in the words of the ancient Gallo-Roman Namatianus, 'into a town' (ibid.).

Virilio's growing awareness of what we might describe as post-terrestrial atmospherics (a phenomenon that has been around since the 1990s) has contributed to his global awareness of a hypercritical space that forces us to register the fallout of critical space in the form of a global region ecologists have totally ignored.

One of the effects of the world-city, Virilio suggests, is that town and countryside find themselves, as we might put it, no longer in opposition. Following a precedent established by the third world, the countryside – the dominant historical space within which Europe, for example, has organized itself for centuries – is threatened by the 'depopulation of a rural space now delivered up to idleness' (Virilio 1997f: 59), under conditions of globalization; it loses its earlier sense of being a productive land and becomes ever more fallow and minute. The end of the town–countryside opposition is not simply an urban effect of hypercritical space's becoming dominant (with its '"intelligence" of the artificial' and lack of concern for either town or countryside). Virilio's growing awareness of what we might describe as post-terrestrial atmospherics (a phenomenon that has been around since the 1990s) has contributed to his global awareness of a hypercritical space that forces us to register the fallout of critical space in the form of a global region ecologists have totally ignored. Virilio gives the example of 'the area of *relativity*, that is, of a new relationship to the places and . . . distances created by the broadcasting revolution, with the recent implementation of . . . electronic radiation' (Virilio 1997f: 60). Within the context of such technological and ecological global changes, Virilio suggests, we are forced increasingly to recognize the end of the town–countryside opposition as a disaster for the human landscape.

The technological and spatial innovativeness associated with hypercritical space is supplanting the idle 'life-size' areas of the world associated with human spatial practices prior to the advent of critical space. For example, nowadays,

> **faced with the decline in geography, now converted into an abstract *science of space*, and the disappearance of exoticism with the boom in tourism and mass communication equipment, surely we should be asking ourselves in all urgency about the meaning and cultural importance of geophysical dimensions.**
>
> **(Virilio 1997f: 60)**

Equally, in the twenty-first century the entirety of the Earth has already been uncovered. The Earth's area is also more homogeneous; critical space, as the techno-instrumentalization of space (which indicates the adaptation of the human body to the mathematization of the natural environment), has been displaced by '*the closed-circuit connection*' (ibid.). The closed-circuit connection prefigures 'the closed-loop connection' and the rise of 'the final looping and locking up of a world that has become *orbital*, not only in terms of circumterrestrial satellites on the beat, but of the entire array of telecommunications tools as well' (Virilio 1997f: 61; see also Armitage 2012: 95–116).

Such increases in the pollution of distances should not be simply equated with a new freedom from terrestrial constraints (although certain critics do make this parallel). For instance, this 'one last form of pollution' has brought with it a new 'concrete reality' and 'the pollution of the geographical expanse', threatening 'the sense of reality we each possess' and the meaning of the world (Virilio 1997f: 61). It has also eroded the *wholeness* of the world – a key feature of gravity, which is in turn associated with a world prior to that of critical space: 'that force of universal attraction that at once lends weight, meaning, and direction to the objects that make up the human environment' (Virilio 1997f: 62). The globalization of 'falling bodies', writes Virilio, 'reveals to all and sundry the *quality* of our environment, its specific weightiness':

> **it is *use* that defines terrestrial space, the environment, we cannot cover any expanse or therefore any (geophysical) 'quantity' except through the effort of more or less lasting (physical) motion, through the fatigue of a journey where the only void that exists exists by nature of the action undertaken in order to cross it.**
>
> **(Virilio 1997f: 62)**

Global hypermovement

If critical space was associated with a spatial dominant – the production of suffering as a form of disappearance – so is hypercritical space, namely with the production of suffering as a form of extreme speed. As Virilio argues, the tendency towards 'superior' global supersonic communication tools is causing the collapse of *all* traditional city, continental, and world spaces. Indeed, these tools are producing such an escalation of space–time, of teletechnological action, of emphasis on the world-city, on the 'territory' of *real-time* telecommunications, on relativity, and on time distances and absolute speed, that I label it *global hypermovement*. The more architecture becomes accelerated by the global hypermovement of speed and time, by the logic of the race, and by globally networked extreme speed and the exceeding of our own limits, the more world space becomes disconnected from specific geographies, expanses, realities, and traditional meanings and appears reduced by technology to the speed of electromagnetic waves.

The feeling of a communal world space, of spatial belonging, becomes progressively harder to sustain within the production of suffering as a form of extreme speed, far removed from any grey ecology. Virilio (1997f: 62) writes of how global hypermovement 'obliterates all direction, the vastness of the earth's horizon', for collectivities conventionally organized around ideas of town and country, earth, gravity, and weight. His use of the term 'direction' here is important. Virilio is not simply contending that we have moved from a time of secure and inert world space to an insecure and accelerated one. Rather, he is suggesting that world space is gradually yielding to a 'new world', where 'proximity has no future'. This last description helps clarify why Virilio's and Tschumi's deconstructive approach to architecture, as seen in the Parc de la Villette, might well flourish in a future where traditional architects, with their seeming confidence in inert world space, might not.

Hyperworld space or the revolution of the hyperevent

Together, hypercritical space and Virilio's theories associated with the production of suffering as a form of extreme speed help explicate why what I term the *revolution of the hyperevent* is so integral to Virilio's conception of grey ecology. The weakening of previous modes of critical space is associated with the waning of traditional ideas of space, territory, location, and world. The consequence is that collective cultural events – bound together by gravity or town or country – become more insecure and accelerated. Hypercritical space realigns the event in new ways, as the technologies of real time, interactive telecommunication, and so on network people and events in ever more closed circuits or limited ways, which are no longer necessarily established by orientation or town and country but develop globally and bewilderingly. Moreover, the production of suffering as a form of extreme speed, alongside the disappearance of all indicators of position and location in the era of the hyperevent, suggests that it is not just our shared feeling of world space that is becoming regressive, meaningless, and insecure.

Additionally, such reversion, futility, and anxiety is destroying the very possibility of a *point of view* and defining a new *pointlessness of view* as the revolution of the hyperevent.

'In the Cities of the Beyond'

Despite Virilio's concentration, in essays like 'Grey Ecology' and interviews such as 'In the Cities of the Beyond' (Virilio and Armitage 2009), on what

I have titled 'hypercritical space' and 'global hypermovement', we might claim that these are not completely acceptable as explanatory categories for transformations in contemporary urban culture. In the 'Cities of the Beyond' interview, Virilio remarks that he does not feel so much theoretically adrift as theoretically focused on the future of the city. He reflects seriously here on the repercussions of global hypermovement and of theories related to the revolution of the hyperevent for his own thinking on hyperevents as a French 'war child' *already* revolutionized, not to say traumatized, through the Second World War (see Chapter 1). In doing so, he also broaches problems concerning global hypermovement as a global condition. 'I argue that we have arrived at a critical threshold regarding cities', he says, because, 'very simply, today . . . the real time of information and communications technologies surpasses the real space of cities' (Virilio and Armitage 2009: 102). In a similar manner he suggests that global hypermovement makes us aware that 'geopolitical cities are now at an end' (ibid.). Virilio's difficulty with global hypermovement has partially to do with its failure to attend to its own urban beyond and 'meteo-political' deconstructions as a metropolitan discourse that is based 'on a sort of atmospheric politics related to the immediacy, ubiquity, and instantaneity of information and communications technologies' (ibid.). It is noteworthy that, of the contemporary social theorists he mentions in his 'Cities of the Beyond' interview, he does not even speak approvingly of the well-known urban sociologist Saskia Sassen. In contrast to Sassen, Virilio follows the *accelerated* logic of cities; contemporary information, communication, and technoculture are unremittingly fast-tracked, and the speeded-up world is overwhelmingly that of the technoculture of the world-city. Sassen (2001) identified the global city as the logic of the command centres of the global economy in her celebrated book.

For Virilio, hypercritical space and global hypermovement, rather than indicating an absolute break, are *tendencies*. Consider the difference between the 'hyper' of 'global hypermovement' and the 'grey' of 'grey ecology' in this context. The former implies that something is overactive; the latter, as Paul Morand wrote in 1937, suggests that something has just begun to accelerate to the point where its colour is obliterated: 'when a gyroscope is spinning fast', Morand reasoned, 'everything goes grey' (cited in Virilio 1997f: 59). As Virilio comments, the globalizing instantaneity, ubiquity, and immediacy of information and communications technologies based on electromagnetic waves are, in numerous ways, the essence of critical space. Likewise, while hypercritical space has global effects, it is nevertheless entrenched within the advanced technoculture of critical space. Thus Virilio's writings on grey ecology are not strictly governed by the questions provoked by hypercritical space and global hypermovement. He is of the view that we are not, as he might put it, quite yet in the cities of the beyond.

Virilio's contemporary standpoint is that we have tended to contemplate global hypermovement too much in relation to 'polar inertia' (Virilio 2000c), a phrase that I have explained elsewhere as describing that 'state or "location" in which or where people cease to be moving bodies and become instead motionless' (Armitage 2012: 161). In contrast to his previous supposition that global hypermovement leads to inactivity, Virilio argues that this phenomenon and the influence of the real time of interactivity have been highly destructive. For Virilio, global hypermovement involves both inactivity *and* the creation of '*the* new ethereal "place" of the city'; it entails, as he puts it frequently, coming to terms with an indescribable 'place' that appropriates 'all our previous understandings of the reality and materiality of geopolitical cities' (Virilio and Armitage 2009: 103). There has been, then, no clear-cut erosion of the real places of town and countryside; rather, global hypermovement has contributed to the dematerialization of town and countryside as 'geography is replaced' by what Virilio calls 'trajectography'. Global hypermovement involves, for him, a dual movement of polar inertia *and* trajectography. On the one hand, the 'inertial properties of objects are increasingly dismissed'; on the other, and relatedly, we are ever more immersed in 'a trajectory of endless acceleration' that has 'now reached the speed of light' (ibid.). Virilio sees this destructive process demonstrated in 'traceability' – the production of an increasingly computer-tracked controlling gaze, which occurs by means of the electromagnetic waves that carry the messages of our suitably named 'cell' phones (Virilio and Armitage 2009: 104). When Virilio (or Tschumi) speak of trajectories or of movement, they are often posing questions such as 'What is a space?', 'What is movement?', 'What is an event?', and 'What is inertia?' Thus the advance of global hypermovement has produced a world-city of movement, which, as we have seen, is an important element in society's becoming 'entirely a function of time', as Tschumi (2000: viii) explained.

What is distinctive about Virilio's explanation of the new grey ecology in the cities of the beyond is how he takes up the issues of global hypermovement presented by the question of hypercritical space. Certainly, for Virilio, something 'is at work here that is truly extraordinary. To be sure, it is the idea that, henceforth, cities are, as the English architects of the Archigram group of the 1960s used to argue, "instant cities"' (Tschumi 2000: viii; see also Crompton 2012). While in relation to the overexposed city we have previously understood that there were significant technological developments since the 1980s (see Chapter 3), the past decade has seen a rapid expansion in such cities (partially because of the rise of the world-city delineated above). It is not just the rise of ethereal, almost spectral, cities and 'places' that has disrupted earlier notions of town and country in this context, but also the fact that 'the structures of geopolitical cities are being replaced by trajectories, by acceleration, and by the gesticulations of traceability' (Virilio and Armitage 2009: 104). We have to remember that, for Virilio, the controlling gaze has not been globalized only by the huge dispersion of automated vision technologies into the world-city, but also by what I have named elsewhere the 'terrorphone' (Armitage 2014) or the techniques of state-sanctioned telephonic pursuit of individuals through the mobile phone.

The globalization of computerized vision technologies, Virilio comments, has not merely incorporated the techniques of pursuit opened up by these new developments. For electronic vision technologies have to work with, through, and around 'the coming megalopolises of 30 to 40 – or even 50 million plus inhabitants', which 'are the real future of the cities of the beyond' (Virilio and Armitage 2009: 104). For example, Virilio argues that the emergent world-city is no longer based on the once powerful, once dominant, once highly futuristic, but now fading overexposed city of the era of critical space, of the age before the arrival of world space. However, side by side with world space is the new future of sensors, cameras, and location-aware devices such as mobile phones. Nongovernmental organizations like Christian Aid and the United Nations have recently spoken of future megalopolises containing 70 million inhabitants, for example, New Delhi in 50 years' time (ibid.). Currently the appearance of megalopolises and the end of geopolitical cities – in fact their disappearance – are a sign of the times in nongovernmental organizations. Here 'the appearance of instantaneous electromagnetic cities, of cities founded on waves', on global hypermovement and inertia, and on the immediacy and ubiquity of information and communications technologies has become the latest development, one that Virilio has been quick to pick upon (ibid.). Some of the spatial and temporal constants once taken for granted, from the night sky and the human-centred horizon to sunrise and sunset, worlds that appeared before the world-city, are being reconfigured and made over into instant cities of interactivity. Virilio does not mistake this new interest in techniques of pursuit for a dystopian placelessness, even if, for example, the concept and the evolving reality of the world-city abolish the very idea of the capital city. But he does say that the 'supersession of real space by real-time information and communications technologies is . . . a break without precedent and one of the key transformative spatiotemporal shifts of the twenty-first century' (Virilio and Armitage 2009: 104). The world-city may work through techniques of pursuit, but those techniques also get absorbed into the prevailing culture of virtual places, while simultaneously obscuring the increasing disappearance of cities we once truly inhabited. As Virilio highlights, it is vital to remember that we are not only facing a new future of mobile phones but also a new future of mobile phone *screens* that complement our ever more dislocated existence.

Some of the spatial and temporal constants once taken for granted, from the night sky and the human-centred horizon to sunrise and sunset, worlds that appeared before the world-city, are being reconfigured and made over into instant cities of interactivity.

Virilio remarks that different yet equally momentous technological developments are also coming into view, narrating the course of globalized and programmed vision technologies from a different perspective, through urban and, crucially, *corporeal* technological trajectories. These hyperevents imply another corporeal 'place' to stand in on the viewing of mobile phone screens, another 'place' to speak from on the subject of our bodies and lives, which are progressively separated from our former houses and lives in the geopolitical city. Virilio's interview continues by considering how these different aspects of the accelerated world-city, as a *new form of city*, produce 'post-sedentary' men and women who are now *at home everywhere* – very much in accordance with Tschumi's idea of contemporary society's becoming completely a function of time:

> **Whether we are on a train or in an airplane, it no longer matters. This is because our 'place' of residence is, thanks to the mobile phone revolution, *everywhere*. Yet, like nomads, we are *at home both everywhere and nowhere*, and, I would suggest, seemingly permanently veering off track.**
>
> **(Virilio and Armitage 2009: 105)**

The disaster that the human landscape described here represents is similar to the one Virilio and Tschumi associate with contemporary space, movement, and the event discussed in the opening sections of this chapter. Our need for a grey ecology arises out of the recognition not only of the new techniques of pursuit, but also of mobile phone-induced *placelessness*. We are now everywhere, nomadic, and global rather than somewhere. We are *swerving off course* and intoxicated as 'accidental choreographers' (ibid.). It is this view of world space as an instantaneous electromagnetic city that is becoming predominant in Virilio's writing on what I have termed hyperspace, hypermovement, and the revolution of the hyperevent.

Thinking differently: grey ecology and the question concerning the contemporary world-city

Virilio maintains that, in the twenty-first century, the regeneration of architecture cannot happen if architects continue to think and act in the same old ways; it has to start with their learning from the lessons taught by Virilio and

Tschumi. Since the beginning of the new millennium, younger architects like Neil Leach (2000) and Adam Sharr (2011), as well as architectural scholars like Mari Lending (2009), Lee Stickells (2010), and Annette Svaneklink Jakobsen (2012), under Virilio and Tschumi's influence, are learning those lessons very well. Focusing on Architecture Principe and on the architecture of Peter Zumthor, on Tschumi's New Acropolis Museum in Athens, on innovative architectural conceptions of ramped surfaces, and on the experience of in-between spaces, movements, and events, these architect-scholars are very conscious of the importance of intervening in debates over the world-city, which is fundamental to Virilio and Tschumi's field of vision. According to Virilio, however, so far these debates have been an effort not so much to formulate a grey ecology for architecture as to celebrate the spatio-temporal realm of the audio-visible. In the era of the mobile phone, Virilio speaks of the hazard of pedestrians no longer seeing anything in front of them. Not for the first time, his remarks on contemporary mobile phone practices appear germane. In his 2009 interview, 'In the Cities of the Beyond', Virilio asked the question: 'What do these mobile phone practices tell us about contemporary cities?' (Virilio and Armitage 2009: 105). It is up to us, as fellow architectural scholars of the cities of the beyond, to seek to answer such questions.

This final chapter began by emphasizing the disjunctions between use, form, and social values in Tschumi's 'A Manifesto of a Different Type' – as well as the achievements of his way of architectural thinking, which I have entitled Tschumism. Through the example of the relation between the three levels of space, movement, and event, we noted one of the key elements of Tschumi's Virilio-influenced mode of architectural thought: space is increasingly overcome by time. Tschumi's central argument in relation to the three levels of space, movement, and event is that his own architectural work, much like Virilio's, is a deconstructive project characterized by society's becoming entirely a function of time, and this is exemplified in Tschumi's Parc de la Villette in Paris. We contemplated the implications of deconstructive architectural ideas for deceptively stable spatial conditions as ever more unstable deconstructive events, which, Tschumi and Virilio argue, traditional architects have failed to take sufficiently into account.

In the second part of the chapter we considered Virilio's grey ecology project and its call for architects to concentrate on the pollution of life-size that is relegating to zero the earth's scale and size. Virilio suggests that his is essentially a response to historic changes in our natural surroundings, to the proximity of human groups, and to ecology in the twenty-first century, and that there is nothing inherently opposed to green ecology in his grey ecology. Through an examination of hypercritical space and global hypermovement, we investigated Virilio's stance on the latter and its implications for architecture in the age of hyperworld space. Where one response to global hypermovement is to reject the inertial properties of things and to submerge ourselves in a trajectory of limitless acceleration that has now touched the speed of light, Virilio suggests a more critical architectural interpretation of world space as an instantaneous electromagnetic city, in response to our obvious need for a grey ecology.

In conclusion, it should be noted that Virilio's writings on grey ecology and the city have proved contentious, receiving criticism, for example, from cultural geographers such as Nigel Thrift (2011). Thrift has many problems with Virilio's project, but let us underline two. First, he thinks that Virilio gives unwarranted emphasis to cities as shapeless agglomerations. Second and relatedly, he argues that Virilio minimizes the irreducible density and specificity of ordinary people, who cannot be interpreted through grand theory alone. We can only wait to see if Virilio offers a response to such criticisms in his future work.

Further reading

English translations of Virilio's key texts are widely available. A substantial (if not complete) inventory of his books in English, together with an extensive catalogue of his articles and interviews and of secondary literature on him, all in English, can be found in my edited volume *The Virilio Dictionary* (Armitage 2013).

For readers seeking to research further into Virilio's architectural thinking, numerous texts are obtainable. My edited book *Paul Virilio: From Modernism to Hypermodernism and Beyond* (Armitage 2000) contains 'Virilio and Architecture' by Neil Leach. Part II ('On Architecture') of my edited volume *Virilio Live: Selected Interviews* (Armitage 2001) includes the interviews 'Paul Virilio and the Oblique' by Enrique Limon and 'The Time of the Trajectory' by Andreas Ruby. My edited text *Virilio Now: Current Perspectives in Virilio Studies* (Armitage 2011) features Adam Sharr's 'Burning Bruder Klaus: Towards an Architecture of Slipstream' on Virilio and the Swiss architect Peter Zumthor.

Beyond architecture, there is my monograph *Virilio and the Media* (Armitage 2012), on Virilio's multifaceted yet fertile notions of aesthetics and cinema, war, new media, and the city. Perhaps the best collection of studies on Virilio's association with art and imagery is the volume *Virilio and Visual Culture* (Armitage and Bishop 2013). The contributors are media and literary theorists, artists, and critical and cultural theorists who reveal the complexity of Virilio's theoretical ideas about painting, perception, and time.

James Der Derian's edited volume *The Virilio Reader* (Der Derian 1998) and Steve Redhead's selection of edited texts in *The Paul Virilio Reader* (Redhead 2004b) chronicle Virilio's career as an architect and urbanist through film, military conflict, and twentieth-century history. Both books position Virilio's philosophy in its French intellectual context and present surveys of his theoretical writings inclusive of their relationship with architecture.

Scholars of French similarly employ Virilio's work, and of particular value to French studies is Ian James' demanding but satisfying monograph *Paul Virilio* (James 2007), which is the preferred source of authority in this field.

Finally, Steve Redhead's monograph *Paul Virilio: Theorist for an Accelerated Culture* (Redhead 2004a) presents an overview of the important themes in Virilio's work on cultural theory. Redhead valuably appraises Virilio's philosophical writings on speed, modernity, and the accident.

Bibliography

Books and articles

Andermatt Conley, Verena (2013) 'Critical Space'. In John Armitage (ed.), *The Virilio Dictionary*. Edinburgh: Edinburgh University Press, pp. 55–8.

Armitage, John (ed.) (2000) *Paul Virilio: From Modernism to Hypermodernism and Beyond*. London: Sage.

Armitage, John (ed.) (2001) *Virilio Live: Selected Interviews*. London: Sage.

Armitage, John (2010) 'Temporary Authoritarian Zone'. In Sarai Collective (ed.), *Sarai Reader 08: Fear*. New Delhi: Centre for the Study of Developing Societies, pp. 18–19.

Armitage, John (ed.) (2011) *Virilio Now: Current Perspectives in Virilio Studies*. Cambridge: Polity.

Armitage, John (2012) *Virilio and the Media*. Cambridge: Polity.

Armitage, John (ed.) (2013) *The Virilio Dictionary*. Edinburgh: Edinburgh University Press.

Armitage, John (2014) 'Terrorphone'. *Journal of Visual Culture* 13 (1): 17–19.

Armitage, John and Bishop, Ryan (eds) (2013) *Virilio and Visual Culture*. Edinburgh: Edinburgh University Press.

Armitage, John and Roberts, Joanne (2007) 'On the Eventuality of Total Destruction'. *City* 11 (3): 428–32.

Banham, Reyner (1966) *The New Brutalism: Ethic or Aesthetic?* London: Architectural Press.

Beck, John (2011) 'Concrete Ambivalence: Inside the Bunker Complex'. *Cultural Politics* 7 (1): 79–102.

Benjamin, Walter (1971) *L'Homme, le langage et la culture*. Paris: Denöel.

Blake, William ([1790] 2000) *The Marriage of Heaven and Hell*. New York: Dover Publications.

Busbea, Larry (2007) *Topologies: The Urban Utopia in France, 1960–1970*. Cambridge, MA: MIT Press.

Caradonna, Jeremy (2012) *The Enlightenment in Practice: Academic Prize Contests and Intellectual Culture in France, 1670–1794*. Ithaca, NY: Cornell University Press.

Crompton, Dennis (2012) *A Guide to Archigram 1961–74*. Princeton, NJ: Princeton Architectural Press.

Debray, Régis (2004) *Transmitting Culture*. New York: Columbia University Press.

Der Derian, James (ed.) (1998) *The Virilio Reader*. Oxford: Blackwell.

Duffy, Enda (2009) *The Speed Handbook: Velocity, Pleasure, Modernism*. Durham, NC: Duke University Press.

Elliott, Brian (2010) *Benjamin for Architects*. London: Routledge.

Fishman, Robert (1982) *Urban Utopias in the Twentieth Century: Ebenezer Howard, Frank Lloyd Wright, Le Corbusier*. Cambridge, MA: MIT Press.

Foucault, Michel (1986) 'Of Other Spaces'. *Diacritics* 16 (1): 22–7.

Gibson, William (1984) *Neuromancer*. New York: Harper Voyager.

Jakobsen, Annette Svaneklink (2012) 'Experience in-between Architecture and Context: The New Acropolis Museum, Athens'. *Journal of Aesthetics and Culture* 4: 1–8.

James, Ian (2007) *Paul Virilio*. London: Routledge.

Kenzari, Bechir (ed.) (2011) *Architecture and Violence*. London: Actar.

Le Corbusier (2008) *Vers une architecture*. Paris: Éditions Flammarion.

Leach, Neil (2000) 'Virilio and Architecture'. In John Armitage (ed.), *Paul Virilio: From Modernism to Hypermodernism and Beyond*. London: Sage, pp. 71–84.

Lefebvre, Henri (1991) *The Production of Space*. Oxford: Wiley Blackwell.

Lending, Mari (2009) 'Negotiating Absence: Bernard Tschumi's New Acropolis Museum in Athens'. *The Journal of Architecture* 14 (5): 567–89.

Lesnikowski, Wojciech (1990) *The New French Architecture*. New York: Rizzoli.

Louppe, Laurence (ed.) (1994) *Traces of Dance*. Paris: Dis Voir.

Lucan, Jacques (1996) 'Introduction'. In Paul Virilio and Claude Parent, *The Function of the Oblique*, trans. Pamela Johnston. London: Architectural Association, pp. 5–10.

Mallgrave, Harry Francis and Goodman, David (2011) *An Introduction to Architectural Theory: 1968 to the Present*. Oxford: Wiley Blackwell.

Mandelbrot, Benoît B. (1982) *The Fractal Geometry of Nature*. New York: W. H. Freeman.

Mandour, M. Alaa (2010) *E-urban: Virtual Urban Spaces*. Berlin: VDM Verlag Dr Müller.

Parent, Claude (1996) 'Projects: Church of Saint-Bernadette du Banlay, Nevers'. In Paul Virilio and Claude Parent, *The Function of the Oblique*, trans. Pamela Johnston. London: Architectural Association, pp. 17–19.

Parent, Claude (1997a) 'Dominating the Site'. In Paul Virilio and Claude Parent, *Architecture Principe 1966 and 1996*, trans. George Collins. Besançon: Les Éditions de l'Imprimeur, p. iv.

Parent, Claude (1997b) 'Structure'. In Paul Virilio and Claude Parent, *Architecture Principe 1966 and 1996*, trans. George Collins. Besançon: Les Éditions de l'Imprimeur, pp. x–xi.

Parent, Claude (1997c) 'The Turbines'. In Paul Virilio and Claude Parent, *Architecture Principe 1966 and 1996*, trans. George Collins. Besançon: Les Éditions de l'Imprimeur, pp. iii–iv.

Perec, Georges (1997) *Species of Spaces and Other Pieces*. London: Penguin.

Redhead, Steve (2004a) *Paul Virilio: Theorist for an Accelerated Culture*. Edinburgh. Edinburgh University Press.

Redhead, Steve (ed.) (2004b) *The Paul Virilio Reader*. New York: Columbia University Press.

Rowe, Colin and Koetter, Fred (1978) *Collage City*. Cambridge, MA: MIT Press.

Sassen, Saskia (2001) *The Global City: New York, London, Tokyo*. Princeton, NJ: Princeton Architectural Press.

Scalbert, Irénée and Mostafavi, Mohsen (1996) 'Interview with Claude Parent'. In Paul Virilio and Claude Parent, *The Function of the Oblique*, trans. Pamela Johnston. London: Architectural Association, pp. 49–58.

Sereny, Gitta (1996) *Albert Speer: His Battle with Truth*. London: Picador.

Sharr, Adam (2011) 'Burning Bruder Klaus: Towards an Architecture of Slipstream'. In John Armitage (ed.), *Virilio Now: Current Perspectives in Virilio Studies*. Cambridge: Polity, pp. 46–67.

Speer, Albert (2003) *Inside the Third Reich*. New York: Phoenix.

Stickells, Lee (2010) 'Conceiving an Architecture of Movement'. *Architectural Research Quarterly* 14 (1): 41–51.

Sudjic, Deyan (2011) *The Edifice Complex: The Architecture of Power*. London: Penguin.

Thrift, Nigel (2011) 'Panicsville: Paul Virilio and the Aesthetic of Disaster'. In John Armitage (ed.), *Virilio Now: Current Perspectives in Virilio Studies*. Cambridge: Polity, pp. 145–57.

Tschumi, Bernard (1981) *The Manhattan Transcripts: Theoretical Projects*. New York: St Martin's Press.

Tschumi, Bernard (1996a) *Architecture and Disjunction*. Cambridge, MA: MIT Press.

Tschumi, Bernard (1996b) 'A Manifesto of a Different Type'. In Paul Virilio and Claude Parent, *Architecture Principe 1966 and 1996*, trans. George Collins. Besançon: Les Éditions de l'Imprimeur, pp. 190–3.

Tschumi, Bernard (2000) 'Foreword'. In Paul Virilio, *A Landscape of Events*, trans. Julie Rose. Princeton, NJ: Princeton Architectural Press, pp. viii–ix.

Tschumi, Bernard and Eisenschmidt, Alexander (2012) 'Importing the City into Architecture: An Interview with Bernard Tschumi'. *Architectural Design* 82 (5): 130–5.

United Nations High Commission for Refugees (UNHCR) (2014) 'Global Facts and Figures', at www.unhcr.org.uk/about-us/key-facts-and-figures.html (accessed 31 March 2014).

Venturi, Robert (1984) *Complexity and Contradiction in Architecture*. New York: Museum of Modern Art.

Verhulst, Ferdinand (2012) *Henri Poincaré: Impatient Genius*. Berlin: Springer.

Virilio, Paul (1976) *L'Insécurité du territoire*. Paris: Stock.

Virilio, Paul (1986) *Speed & Politics: An Essay on Dromology*, trans. Mark Polizzotti. New York: Semiotext(e).

Virilio, Paul (1989) *War and Cinema: The Logistics of Perception*, trans. Patrick Camiller. London: Verso.

Virilio, Paul (1990) *Popular Defense and Ecological Struggles*, trans. Mark Polizzotti. New York: Semiotext(e).

Virilio, Paul (1991) *The Lost Dimension*, trans. Daniel Moshenberg. New York: Semiotext(e).

Virilio, Paul (1994a) *Bunker Archeology*, trans. George Collins. Princeton, NJ: Princeton Architectural Press.

Virilio, Paul (1994b) *The Vision Machine*, trans. Julie Rose. London: British Film Institute.

Virilio, Paul (1995) *The Art of the Motor*, trans. Julie Rose. Minneapolis, MN: University of Minnesota Press.

Virilio, Paul (1997a) 'Bunker Archeology'. In Paul Virilio and Claude Parent, *Architecture Principe 1966 and 1996*, trans. George Collins. Besançon: Les Éditions de l'Imprimeur, pp. xvii–xviii.

Virilio, Paul (1997b) 'Disorientation'. In Paul Virilio and Claude Parent, *Architecture Principe 1966 and 1996*, trans. George Collins. Besançon: Les Éditions de l'Imprimeur, pp. 7–14.

Virilio, Paul (1997c) 'Manhattan Out'. In Paul Virilio and Claude Parent, *Architecture Principe 1966 and 1996*, trans. George Collins. Besançon: Les Éditions de l'Imprimeur, pp. v–vi.

Virilio, Paul (1997d) 'The Nevers Work Site'. In Paul Virilio and Claude Parent, *Architecture Principe 1966 and 1996*, trans. George Collins. Besançon: Les Éditions de l'Imprimeur, pp. xi–xii.

Virilio, Paul (1997e) 'The Oblique Function'. In Paul Virilio and Claude Parent, *Architecture Principe 1966 and 1996*, trans. George Collins. Besançon: Les Éditions de l'Imprimeur, p. iii.

Virilio, Paul (1997f) *Open Sky*, trans. Julie Rose. London: Verso.

Virilio, Paul (1997g) 'Warning'. In Paul Virilio and Claude Parent, *Architecture Principe 1966 and 1996*, trans. George Collins. Besançon: Les Éditions de l'Imprimeur, p. iii.

Virilio, Paul (2000a) *The Information Bomb*, trans. Chris Turner. London: Verso.

Virilio, Paul (2000b) *A Landscape of Events*, trans. Julie Rose. Princeton, NJ: Princeton Architectural Press.

Virilio, Paul (2000c) *Polar Inertia*, trans. Patrick Camiller. London: Sage.

Virilio, Paul (2000d) *Strategy of Deception*, trans. Chris Turner. London: Verso.

Virilio, Paul (2002a) *Desert Screen: War at the Speed of Light*, trans. Michael Degener. London: Continuum.

Virilio, Paul (2002b) *Ground Zero*, trans. Chris Turner. London: Verso.

Virilio, Paul (2003a) *Art and Fear*, trans. Julie Rose. London: Continuum.

Virilio, Paul (2003b) *Unknown Quantity*, trans. Chris Turner and Jian-Xing Too. London: Thames & Hudson.

Virilio, Paul (2005a) *City of Panic*, trans. Julie Rose. Oxford: Berg.

Virilio, Paul (2005b) *Negative Horizon*, trans. Michel Degener. London: Continuum.

Virilio, Paul (2007a) *Art as Far as the Eye Can See*, trans. Julie Rose. Oxford: Berg.

Virilio, Paul (2007b) *The Original Accident*, trans. Julie Rose. Cambridge: Polity.

Virilio, Paul (2009a) *The Aesthetics of Disappearance*, trans. Philip Beitchman. New York: Semiotext(e).

Virilio, Paul (2009b) *Grey Ecology*, trans. Drew Burk. New York: Atropos.

Virilio, Paul (2010a) *The Futurism of the Instant: Stop–Eject*, trans. Julie Rose. Cambridge: Polity.

Virilio, Paul (2010b) *The University of Disaster*, trans. Julie Rose. Cambridge: Polity.

Virilio, Paul (2012) *The Great Accelerator*, trans. Julie Rose. Cambridge: Polity.

Virilio, Paul and Armitage, John (2001a) 'From Modernism to Hypermodernism and Beyond'. In John Armitage (ed.), *Virilio Live: Selected Interviews*. London: Sage, pp. 15–47.

Virilio, Paul and Armitage, John (2001b) 'The Kosovo W@r Did Take Place'. In John Armitage (ed.), *Virilio Live: Selected Interviews*. London: Sage, pp. 167–97.

Virilio, Paul and Armitage, John (2009) 'In the Cities of the Beyond: An Interview with Paul Virilio'. In Brigitte van der Sande (ed.), *OPEN 18: 2030: War Zone Amsterdam: Imagining the Unimaginable*. Amsterdam: NAi Publishers-SKOR, pp. 100–11.

Virilio, Paul and Armitage, John (2011) 'The Third War: Cities, Conflict and Contemporary Art: Interview with Paul Virilio'. In John Armitage (ed.), *Virilio Now: Current Perspectives in Virilio Studies*. Cambridge: Polity, pp. 29–45.

Virilio, Paul and Baj, Enrico (2003) *Discurso sobre el horror en el arte*, trans. Giulio Scafa. Madrid: Casimiro Libros.

Virilio, Paul and Brausch, Marianne (1993) 'Marginal Groups'. *Diadalos: Berlin Architectural Journal* 50: 72–81.

Virilio, Paul and Brausch, Marianne (2011) *A Winter's Journey: Four Conversations with Marianne Brausch*, trans. Chris Turner. Chicago, IL: University of Chicago Press.

Virilio, Paul and Brügger, Niels (2001) 'Perception, Politics, and the Intellectual'. In John Armitage (ed.), *Virilio Live: Selected Interviews*. London: Sage, pp. 82–96.

Virilio, Paul and Depardon, Raymond (2008) *Native Land: Stop Eject*. Paris: Actes Sud.

Virilio, Paul and Kittler, Friedrich (2001) 'The Information Bomb: A Conversation'. In John Armitage (ed.), *Virilio Live: Selected Interviews*. London: Sage, pp. 97–112.

Virilio, Paul and Limon, Enrique (2001) 'Paul Virilio and the Oblique'. In John Armitage (ed.), *Virilio Live: Selected Interviews*. London: Sage, pp. 51–7.

Virilio, Paul and Lotringer, Sylvère (2002) *Crepuscular Dawn*, trans. Michael Taormina. New York: Semiotext(e).

Virilio, Paul and Lotringer, Sylvère (2005) *The Accident of Art*, trans. Michael Taormina. New York: Semiotext(e).

Virilio, Paul and Lotringer, Sylvère (2008) *Pure War*, trans. Philip Beitchman, Brian O'Keefe, and Mark Polizzotti. New York: Semiotext(e).

Virilio, Paul and Parent, Claude (1996) *The Function of the Oblique*, trans. Pamela Johnston. London: Architectural Association.

Virilio, Paul and Parent, Claude (1997a) *Architecture Principe 1966 and 1996*, trans. George Collins. Besançon: Les Éditions de l'Imprimeur.

Virilio, Paul and Parent, Claude (1997b) 'Site'. In Paul Virilio and Claude Parent, *Architecture Principe 1966 and 1996*, trans. George Collins. Besançon: Les Éditions de l'Imprimeur, pp. xii–xiii.

Virilio, Paul and Parent, Claude (1997c) 'Technique'. In Paul Virilio and Claude Parent, *Architecture Principe 1966 and 1996*, trans. George Collins. Besançon: Les Éditions de l'Imprimeur, p. xiii.

Virilio, Paul and Petit, Philippe (1999) *The Politics of the Very Worst*. New York: Semiotext(e).

Virilio, Paul and Richard, Bertrand (2012) *The Administration of Fear*. New York: Semiotext(e).

Filmography

Virilio, Paul and Paoli, Stéphane (2009) *Penser la vitesse* (DVD). Paris: Arte.

Index